THE RULE ESTATE

The Ultimate Guide To **Buying**, **Managing** And **Growing** A Real Estate Fortune

Wisdom Kwati

Ordering Details

To place orders or for details of discounts for bulk purchases by organizations or groups either for support, gift, training packages, fundraising, or any other educational purposes, send an email to <u>wisdomkwati@gmail.com</u>.
Visit www.wisdomkwati.com or follow me on @Wisdom Kwati across all social media platforms.

Table of Contents

Chapter 1

What Real Estate Investing Is

I have always loved to know people from across various cultures and each time, there is this feeling that envelops me. It is that feeling of knowing that Africa is growing on all fronts. This was the same feeling I had coming to know about Nairobi, Kenya. In this book, I will share the story of Kwame, a young Kenyan man who desired to do things differently.

Kwame grew up amidst the dynamic landscape of the real estate industry. From a young age, he was captivated by the sight of construction cranes, the hum of building projects, and the transformative power of architecture. As he walked through the streets of his neighborhood, he couldn't help but envision the possibilities of creating beautiful spaces that would shape the lives of individuals and communities.

Kwame came from a modest background, but his determination and passion for real estate burned brightly within him. He devoured books on architecture, urban planning and property development, absorbing every piece of knowledge he could find. He spent hours exploring the city, studying its neighborhoods and envisioning the potential for growth and transformation.

One evening, as Kwame gazed at the stunning skyline of Nairobi, he made a solemn vow to himself. He would dedicate his life to becoming a successful real estate entrepreneur, someone who could not only build magnificent structures but also positively impact the lives of those around him. With his mind set on this ambitious goal, Kwame began his journey into the world of real estate.

Aware of the complexities and challenges of the real estate industry, Kwame knew he needed guidance from someone who had navigated those waters successfully. Through networking events and extensive research, he discovered a renowned real estate tycoon named Mr. Obi. Mr. Obi had built an impressive portfolio of properties across Africa and was known for his innovative strategies and ethical business practices.

With a mixture of excitement and nervousness, Kwame reached out to Mr. Obi, expressing his deep admiration for his achievements and his eagerness to learn from him.

Seeing how passionate Kwame was and his genuine desire to make a difference, Mr. Obi agreed to be his mentor.

Their first meeting was a turning point for Kwame. Mr. Obi shared stories of his own journey, the challenges he faced, and the principles that guided him to success. He stressed the importance of integrity, patience, and meticulous research in the real estate industry.

Over the months that followed, Kwame immersed himself in Mr. Obi's mentorship. They met regularly, discussing market trends, investment strategies, and the importance of community development. Mr. Obi introduced Kwame to his extensive network of industry professionals, providing him with valuable connections and opportunities.

Just like Kwame, you are wondering how you can get started in the real estate industry. But first, I need you to understand that when we talk about Real Estate Investing, we are looking at the acquisition, ownership, management, rental or sale of properties for the purpose of generating income or capital appreciation. It is a popular investment avenue globally, including in Nigeria and other African countries.

Imagine you have some money and you're thinking about where to invest it. Real estate investment is the best option to start with. This way, you are using your money to buy properties like lands, houses or apartments.

Real estate can help you create wealth. When you buy a property, it has the potential to increase in value over time. It's like buying a rare toy that becomes more valuable as time goes on. This increase in value is called appreciation. So, if you sell the property later, you can make a profit and add to your overall wealth.

Another thing about real estate investment is that it can provide you with a steady stream of income. When you own a property, you can rent it out to someone else. It's like having a rental property. The rent you receive from the tenants is the money they pay you to live in the property. This rental income can be a reliable source of cash flow, almost like getting a regular paycheck. And the best part is that you don't have to do much work once the property is set up for renting.

Another benefit of investing in real estate is diversification. You spread out your money into different types of investments, so you're not putting all your eggs in one basket. Real estate is different from other types of investments like stocks or bonds. It's like having a variety of different toys instead of just one.

The value of real estate often doesn't rise and fall in the same way as the stock market or other investments. So, if one type of investment is not doing well, your real estate investment might still be doing fine. This can help reduce the risk of losing all your money at once.

Real estate investment also offers long-term stability. This means that even when the economy is not doing well, owning a property can still bring you a stable income. It's like having a reliable job that continues to pay you, even if there are some ups and downs in the economy.

Additionally, when prices go up and things become more expensive over time (which is called inflation), the value of real estate usually goes up too. So, owning a property can help protect you from the rising prices and keep your money's value safe.

Here is the most interesting part; investing in real estate can have some tax advantages. The government gives you some benefits and deductions to lower the taxes you have to pay on your real estate investment. For example, you can deduct some of the costs of owning and maintaining the property from your taxable income. This helps reduce the amount of money you have to pay in taxes.

Also, when you sell a property that you've owned for a long time and made a profit on, you might be eligible for lower tax rates on that profit. This means you get to keep more of the money you made from selling the property.

Starting Your Real Estate Journey

The real estate market in Nigeria and Africa as a whole has been growing a lot and has a lot of potential for people who want to invest their money. It's just like a garden where plants are growing really fast because they have the right conditions to thrive. That's what real estate investing looks like.

In Nigeria and Africa, there are many factors that contribute to the growth of the real estate market. One reason is that more and more people are moving to cities and need places to live and work. Yes, a lot of people are moving to the city and they will be needing houses and offices.

Another reason is that the population is increasing, which means more people need homes. Imagine having a bigger family and needing a bigger house. It is also no news that the middle class is growing, which means more people have enough money to buy or rent properties. It's like having more people who can afford to buy nice toys.

And finally, more foreign companies are investing in real estate in Nigeria and Africa. Having visitors from other places who want to buy things in your neighborhood opens that place up for investment. That's exactly what real estate does.

In Nigeria specifically, the real estate sector has grown a lot, especially in big cities like Lagos, Abuja, and Port Harcourt. These cities have seen a lot of new buildings for businesses, homes, and apartments because there is a big demand from companies, people coming from other countries, and the growing middle class. It's like having a lot of new stores, houses, and apartments being built because many people want them.

There's also something called Real Estate Investment Trusts (REITs), which are a way for people to invest in real estate without directly owning and managing properties. REITs are like a group of people who pool their money together to buy and manage different types of real estate, such as houses, commercial buildings, or infrastructure projects. A group of people pool their money together to buy different properties and share the profits.

Investing in REITs has a few benefits. One benefit is that it helps spread the risk. This means that if one property or area is not doing well, there are other properties in different places that can still make money.

Another benefit is that you can easily buy or sell shares of REITs on the stock exchange. You can buy or sell parts of an investment whenever you want. Also, REITs have to give a big portion of their profits to the investors as regular payments.

There are also some tax advantages to investing in REITs in Nigeria. This means that you don't have to pay as much in taxes on the money you make from your investment. It's like getting a discount on the toys you buy, so you have more money left over to spend.

But it's important to remember that investing in REITs, like any investment, comes with risks. The value of the shares can go up and down depending on the market, interest rates, and how the real estate market is doing. It's like the price of items changing depending on what other people are willing to pay for them.

So, before investing, it's important to do research, understand the history and financial health of the REIT, and think about how much risk you are willing to take.

Is Investing in Real Estate Ideal?

Investing in real estate can be ideal for many individuals, but it ultimately depends on various factors such as financial goals, risk tolerance, market conditions and personal circumstances.

Real estate can be an effective way to diversify your investment portfolio. It offers an alternative asset class that may have a different risk-return profile compared to traditional investments like stocks and bonds. When you diversify your investments, you can potentially reduce the overall risk in your portfolio.

Real estate investments, particularly rental properties, can provide a steady stream of income through rental payments. This can be especially attractive for individuals seeking regular cash flow or those looking for passive income in retirement.

Historically, real estate has shown the potential for long-term appreciation in value. Property values tend to increase over time, especially in growing markets. This appreciation can contribute to the growth of your wealth.

Real estate can serve as a hedge against inflation. During periods of inflation, property values and rental income have the potential to increase, helping to preserve the purchasing power of your investments.

Real estate investments may offer various tax advantages. For example, you may be eligible for deductions on mortgage interest, property taxes, and depreciation. Additionally, in some countries and jurisdictions, 1031 Exchanges allow you to defer capital gains taxes when selling a property and reinvesting the proceeds into another property.

Unlike some other investment options, real estate provides a tangible asset that you can physically own and control. This can provide a sense of security and hands-on involvement in managing your investment.

Challenges Starting Real Estate Journey

Every person you see excelling in the real estate sector passed through certain challenges along their journey. The path to success in real estate is rarely smooth, and individuals who have achieved great heights in this industry have typically encountered obstacles and difficulties that tested their resilience and determination.

These challenges can arise from various aspects of the real estate business, including market conditions, financial constraints, regulatory hurdles, and personal or professional setbacks.

One of the common challenges in real estate is the ever-changing market dynamics. The real estate market can be unpredictable, with fluctuations in property values, demand and supply. You need to stay updated on market trends, economic indicators and demographic shifts to make informed decisions.

Adapting to market changes, such as shifts in demand for certain types of properties or adjusting strategies during economic downturns, requires flexibility and a keen understanding of the market.

Financial constraints can also pose significant challenges in real estate. Acquiring properties often requires substantial capital, and securing financing can be a hurdle, particularly for individuals starting in the industry. You may face difficulties in obtaining loans or finding suitable investment partners.

Additionally, managing cash flow and dealing with unexpected expenses, such as maintenance or repairs, can strain resources and require careful financial management.

Navigating regulatory frameworks and compliance requirements is another challenge in the real estate sector. Each country or region has its own set of laws and regulations governing property ownership, development, and transactions.

Understanding and adhering to these legal requirements can be complex and time-consuming. Working with legal advisors and professionals who specialize in real estate can help you navigate the intricacies of the regulatory landscape and ensure compliance.

Personal and professional setbacks are also common in the real estate industry. Rejections, failures and setbacks are part of the journey towards success. You may encounter difficulties in negotiations, face obstacles in closing deals or experience setbacks in property development projects. However, overcoming these challenges often leads to personal growth, resilience and the acquisition of valuable skills and knowledge.

It should not surprise you to know that the real estate industry demands persistence, patience and a long-term mindset. Building a successful real estate career or business requires dedication and perseverance. It may take time to establish a reputation, build a network of contacts and cultivate valuable relationships with clients and industry professionals.

Real Estate is capital intensive. Investing in real estate often requires a significant upfront investment. Acquiring properties, financing, and ongoing maintenance can involve substantial costs. It may not be feasible for individuals with limited capital.

We cannot talk about Real Estate without talking about Market Volatility. Real estate markets can be subject to fluctuations and cycles. Economic downturns or changes in local market conditions can impact property values and rental demand, potentially leading to financial losses.

Illiquidity is another thing that characterizes real estate investments. Yes, it can be relatively illiquid compared to other investment options like stocks. Selling a property can take time, and the process may involve transaction costs.

Real estate investment requires active management, including finding and managing tenants, handling repairs and maintenance, and dealing with legal and regulatory obligations. It can be time-consuming and may require specific skills or the engagement of property management services.

When you decide to incest on real estate, consider risk and uncertainty. Real estate investment carries inherent risks, including market risk, tenant defaults, property damage and legal disputes. It's crucial to assess your risk tolerance and be prepared for potential challenges.

While facing challenges in the real estate sector is inevitable, it is how you respond and adapt to these challenges that ultimately determines your success. When you embrace these hurdles as an avenue to learn, seek innovative solutions and maintain a strong work ethic, you will find yourself overcoming them and achieving excellence in the real estate sector.

Ultimately, the suitability of real estate investment depends on your individual financial goals, risk tolerance and personal circumstances. This is why I advise that you conduct thorough research, seek professional advice and carefully evaluate the potential risks and rewards before making any investment decisions.

Start Building A Real Estate Fortune

Building a real estate fortune requires careful planning, diligent execution, and a long-term perspective. I started building mine at a time when I was clear about the industry, even though we get to experience new situations as the day passes. The point is that there are some steps to consider when starting your journey towards building a real estate fortune. They include:

Define Your Financial Goals. Clearly articulate your financial goals and objectives. Determine the specific outcomes you want to achieve through real estate investing, such as generating passive income, achieving long-term capital appreciation or building a portfolio of rental properties.

Educate Yourself. Acquire knowledge about real estate investing. Read books, attend seminars and explore online resources to gain a solid understanding of real estate fundamentals, investment strategies, market analysis, financing options and legal considerations. Continuous learning is essential for making informed investment decisions.

Build a Strong Financial Foundation. Before diving into real estate investing, establish a strong financial foundation. Pay off high-interest debt, save for an emergency fund, and ensure you have a good credit score. Having a stable financial base will increase your borrowing capacity and reduce financial stress when starting your real estate ventures.

Set a Realistic Budget. Determine the amount of capital you are willing and able to invest in real estate. Create a budget that considers both acquisition costs and ongoing expenses such as property maintenance, taxes, insurance and potential vacancies. Ensure that your budget aligns with your financial capabilities and goals.

Define Your Investment Strategy. A lot of people jump into Real Estate without having a strategy. You must decide on a specific investment strategy based on your goals, risk tolerance and market conditions. Consider options such as rental properties, fix-and-flip projects, commercial real estate, or real estate investment trusts (REITs). Each strategy has its own characteristics and requires a different level of involvement, so choose the one that suits your resources and preferences.

Conduct Market Research. Thoroughly analyze the real estate market in your target location. Assess factors such as population growth, economic indicators, job opportunities, infrastructure development and rental demand. Identify areas with potential for growth and profitability. Networking with other local real estate professionals can provide valuable insights into market dynamics.

Secure Financing. Explore financing options to fund your real estate investments. This may include traditional bank loans, private lenders, partnerships or utilizing your own savings. Evaluate the terms, interest rates and repayment schedules to select the most suitable financing option for your investment strategy.

Start Small and Learn. Begin with smaller, manageable investments to gain experience and build confidence. Consider starting with a single rental property or a modest fix-and-flip project. Learn the intricacies of property management, tenant selection, renovation and deal analysis. Use these early investments as learning opportunities to refine your strategies and processes.

Network and Collaborate. Build a strong network of real estate professionals, including agents, contractors, property managers, and fellow investors. Attend industry events, join real estate investment groups, and engage in online communities to connect with like-minded individuals.

Collaborating with experienced professionals can provide valuable guidance, access to deals and opportunities for growth.

Continuous Evaluation and Adaptation. Regularly review and evaluate your real estate investments. Track the performance of your properties, analyze cash flow and assess the market conditions. Be willing to adapt your strategies based on changing market dynamics and lessons learned from previous investments.

Scale and Diversify. As you gain experience and confidence, gradually scale your real estate portfolio. Consider diversifying across different property types, locations and investment strategies. Diversification helps mitigate risks and potentially enhances returns.

Seek Professional Advice. Engage professionals such as real estate attorneys, tax advisors and property managers to ensure compliance with legal and regulatory requirements, optimize tax benefits and streamline property management operations. Their expertise can help protect your investments and optimize financial outcomes.

Dealing With Market Fluctuations

Building a real estate fortune requires patience, perseverance and a long-term perspective. It is essential to remain disciplined and committed to your investment strategy, even during market fluctuations. To achieve this, you must take the right actions and build the right skills.

Emphasize Property Due Diligence. Conduct thorough due diligence on potential properties before making a purchase. Evaluate factors such as location, property condition, rental demand, comparable sales and potential renovation costs. Engage professionals for property inspections and legal reviews to uncover any hidden issues or risks.

Develop Negotiation Skills. Negotiation plays a vital role in real estate investing. Hone your negotiation skills to secure favorable purchase prices, financing terms and vendor contracts. Learning effective negotiation techniques can help you maximize your returns and create more opportunities.

Leverage Technology and Data. Stay informed and leverage technology and data to enhance your decision-making process. Utilize real estate investment software, online listing platforms, and data analytics tools to analyze market trends, property performance and investment opportunities. This can provide valuable insights for making informed investment decisions.

Optimize Property Management. Effective property management is crucial for maximizing returns and minimizing vacancies. Develop efficient systems for tenant screening, rent collection, property maintenance and responding to tenant inquiries. Alternatively, consider outsourcing property management to experienced professionals if it aligns with your investment strategy.

Reinvest Profits. As your real estate portfolio grows, consider reinvesting profits into acquiring additional properties or funding larger projects. Reinvesting allows you to compound your returns and accelerate wealth creation. Develop a systematic approach for allocating profits towards future investments.

Monitor and Adjust Financing. Regularly review your financing options to ensure you have the most favorable terms for your investments. As your portfolio expands, explore refinancing options to lower interest rates or access equity for further investment. Keep a keen eye on market trends and changes in lending conditions.

Stay Abreast of Market Trends. Continuously educate yourself on market trends, legal and regulatory changes and emerging investment opportunities. Subscribe to industry publications, follow real estate news and attend industry events to stay updated. Being proactive and adaptable to market dynamics can give you a competitive advantage.

Seek Professional Growth. Invest in your own professional development as a real estate investor. Consider obtaining relevant certifications, attending advanced training programs or joining mentorship programs. Continuously expanding your knowledge and skills can enhance your ability to identify and capitalize on lucrative investment opportunities.

Remember, building a real estate fortune takes time, dedication and a willingness to learn from both successes and failures. While there are risks involved, a well-executed real estate investment strategy has the potential to create long-term wealth and financial independence.

Chapter 2

Developing a Real Estate Investment Strategy

Do you remember Kwame in Chapter 1? Kwame has decided to go into Real Estate Investing. Now, he understood that to succeed in the real estate industry, he needed to acquire knowledge and skills beyond what his mentor could provide. He enrolled in real estate courses, both online and at a local university, to deepen his understanding of property acquisition, financial analysis and property management.

He also attended seminars, workshops and industry conferences, where he had the opportunity to learn from seasoned professionals and gain insights into the ever-evolving dynamics of the real estate market. Kwame devoured books written by renowned real estate experts, studying their strategies and philosophies.

To gain practical experience, he sought internships and volunteer opportunities at local real estate firms. He spent time shadowing property managers, architects and construction teams, absorbing knowledge from every aspect of the industry. Kwame's dedication to learning and preparing himself for success set him apart from his peers.

With a solid foundation of knowledge and the guidance of his mentor, Kwame felt ready to make his first real estate investment. He knew that careful market research and analysis were crucial for identifying a property with potential.

Kwame spent countless hours studying market trends, analyzing property values, and evaluating the growth potential of different neighborhoods. He visited properties, inspecting them meticulously and envisioning their transformation.

It was during one of Kwame's property visits that he stumbled upon a neglected building in an up-and-coming neighborhood called Greenfield Heights. The neighborhood had recently undergone infrastructure improvements and was attracting attention from investors and young professionals looking for affordable housing options.

Kwame saw the potential in the building. Its architecture had a unique charm, and its location was prime for redevelopment. Excitement coursed through his veins as he imagined the possibilities of transforming it into a modern, vibrant residential complex.

Eager to seize the opportunity, Kwame conducted thorough due diligence. He researched the property's history, zoning regulations and potential rental demand in the area. He consulted with architects and contractors to estimate the costs of renovation and refurbishment.

Armed with comprehensive knowledge and a well-thought-out plan, Kwame approached the property owner, Mr. Kamau, to negotiate a deal. He presented his vision for the building, highlighting the potential for growth and increased property value. Kwame's confidence and genuine passion for revitalizing the neighborhood convinced Mr. Kamau to sell the property at a reasonable price.

With the help of his mentor, Kwame secured a loan from a local bank to finance the purchase and renovation costs. The bank recognised his dedication and preparation, viewing him as a promising entrepreneur with a solid investment plan. He knew this project was going to be a hit as he had a solid investment strategy at hand.

Developing A Real Estate Investment Strategy

Developing a real estate investment strategy is like planning a road trip to a destination you've never been to before. You will need a strategy. Having a strategy helps you set clear goals for your investment. It's like deciding the purpose of your trip—whether it's to have fun, explore new places, or reach a specific destination. Setting clear goals allows you to make informed decisions that align with what you want to achieve and helps you stay focused on reaching those goals.

Secondly, a good investment strategy helps you manage risks, just like taking precautions during your road trip. When you do your research and understand the potential risks involved in specific investment opportunities, you can take measures to minimize those risks. It's like packing a spare tire, checking the weather forecast, or having a backup plan in case something goes wrong. Managing risks protects your investment and reduces the chances of losses.

Furthermore, an investment strategy acts as a decision-making guide. Just like a roadmap helps you decide which turns to take during your trip, a strategy helps you evaluate and prioritize investment opportunities based on your goals and risk tolerance. With a strategy in place, you can make informed decisions and avoid impulsive choices that might steer you away from your long-term objectives.

Maximizing returns is another benefit of having an investment strategy. Just like planning your trip to include exciting destinations and activities, a strategy helps you identify lucrative investment opportunities that have the potential to generate higher returns. This way, you can make the most of your investments and increase your chances of achieving your financial goals.

Long-term planning is crucial in real estate investing, and a strategy helps you plan ahead. It's like planning your trip itinerary and knowing where you'll be staying each night. By defining your investment timeline, exit strategies, and plans for expanding or diversifying your portfolio, you can navigate market changes and take advantage of opportunities that align with your strategy.

Consistency and discipline are essential in real estate investing, just like sticking to your planned route during a road trip. An investment strategy provides a structured approach, helping you stay focused on your long-term goals. It prevents you from being influenced by short-term market fluctuations or making impulsive decisions that could hurt your investments.

Additionally, an investment strategy allows you to adapt to market changes, similar to adjusting your travel plans based on road conditions or weather. Real estate markets can be influenced by economic factors, regulations, and demographic shifts. Having a well-defined strategy helps you monitor market trends, adjust your investment approach, and capitalize on emerging opportunities while mitigating risks.

An investment strategy also helps you overcome emotional biases. Emotions can cloud judgment during investment decisions. Having a structured approach based on research, analysis, and predetermined criteria helps you make more rational investment decisions, reducing the impact of emotional biases.

Moreover, developing an investment strategy demonstrates professionalism and seriousness as an investor. Having an investment strategy tells others that you approach your investments thoughtfully. It builds credibility, fosters relationships, and opens doors to collaboration or financing opportunities.

Finally, an investment strategy allows you to track your progress and hold yourself accountable, similar to using a map or GPS to track your trip. It provides a benchmark to measure the performance of your investments, evaluate the effectiveness of your strategy, and make adjustments when needed. This ensures that you're continuously working towards your financial goals and maximizing your investment outcomes.

Steps To Consider When Crafting Your Strategy

Developing a comprehensive real estate investment strategy is essential for achieving your financial goals and maximizing returns. Here are key steps to consider when crafting your strategy:

Assess Your Financial Capacity and Risk Tolerance. Evaluate your financial situation, including your income, savings and overall financial stability. Determine the amount of capital you can allocate to real estate investments without compromising your financial well-being. Consider your risk tolerance, which reflects your willingness and ability to withstand potential financial losses. Assessing your financial capacity and risk tolerance will help shape your investment approach.

Define Your Investment Objectives. Clearly articulate your investment objectives. Are you seeking long-term capital appreciation, regular rental income or a combination of both? Determine the desired rate of return on your investments and establish specific goals that align with your financial aspirations. Defining your objectives will guide your decision-making process and help you focus on investments that align with your goals.

Set a Realistic Timeline. Real estate investments typically require a long-term commitment. Consider your investment horizon and determine the timeline for achieving your financial objectives. Set realistic expectations regarding the time it may take to build wealth through real estate. Your timeline will influence the types of investments you pursue and the strategies you employ.

Conduct Market Research. Thorough market research is crucial for identifying lucrative investment opportunities. Analyze both macro and microeconomic factors that influence the real estate market. Evaluate local market conditions, including population growth, employment rates, infrastructure development and rental demand. Identify emerging trends and areas with high growth potential. A deep understanding of the market will enable you to make informed investment decisions.

Identify Investment Opportunities. Based on your market research, identify specific investment opportunities that align with your strategy and objectives. Consider different types of real estate, such as residential, commercial, industrial or mixed-use properties. Assess the potential risks and returns associated with each investment opportunity. Evaluate factors such as location, property condition, rental income potential, and market demand. Conduct thorough due diligence before finalizing any investment decision.

Understand Risk Management and Diversification. Manage risk by diversifying your real estate portfolio. Avoid putting all your investments in a single property or location. Consider diversifying across different types of properties and geographic areas to reduce exposure to specific market risks. Additionally, establish contingency plans and maintain adequate reserves for unexpected expenses or vacancies.

Create an Exit Strategy. Include an exit strategy in your investment plan. Determine how and when you will exit an investment to realize profits or mitigate losses. Options may include selling a property, refinancing, or exchanging it for another investment. Having a clear exit strategy helps you stay focused on your long-term objectives and ensures you can make informed decisions when the time comes.

Engage in Regular Evaluation and Adjustment. Continuously monitor and evaluate your investment portfolio. Regularly review the performance of your properties, market trends, and changes in investment conditions. Be prepared to adjust your strategy if necessary based on new opportunities or market shifts. Flexibility and adaptability are key to long-term success in real estate investing.

Seek Professional Guidance. Consider working with real estate professionals who can provide valuable expertise and guidance throughout your investment journey. Engage the services of real estate agents, property managers, attorneys, and financial advisors with experience in real estate investment. They can help you navigate complex legal and financial matters, provide market insights, and assist with property management, ensuring your investments are optimized.

Develop a Network. Build a strong network of professionals and fellow investors within the real estate industry. Attend networking events, join investment groups, and participate in online forums to connect with like-minded individuals. Networking can provide access to potential partnerships, deal opportunities, and valuable industry knowledge.

Seek Continual Education. Stay abreast of industry trends, changes in regulations, and new investment strategies through continuous education. Attend seminars, workshops, and conferences related to real estate investing. Read books, subscribe to industry publications, and follow reputable online sources. By continuously expanding your knowledge, you'll be better equipped to make informed decisions and adapt to market dynamics.

Monitor Financing Options. Regularly review financing options to ensure you have access to favorable terms and rates. Stay informed about lending conditions, interest rates, and loan programs. Explore different financing sources, including traditional banks, private lenders, crowdfunding platforms, and government-backed loan programs. Optimizing your financing can significantly impact your investment returns.

Evaluate Tax Implications. Understand the tax implications of your real estate investments. Consult with tax professionals to ensure you maximize available tax benefits, deductions, and incentives. Familiarize yourself with tax regulations specific to real estate, such as depreciation, 1031 exchanges, and capital gains taxes. Proper tax planning can enhance your overall investment returns.

Monitor and Adjust Your Strategy. Regularly review and assess the performance of your investment portfolio. Track cash flows, rental income, expenses, and property appreciation. Analyze the effectiveness of your investment strategy and adjust as necessary. Be prepared to sell underperforming properties, reallocate resources, or explore new investment opportunities based on market conditions and your financial objectives.

Finally, determine your investment approach. If you're planning to invest in real estate, there are different ways you can approach it. Choosing the right investment approach is important because it determines how you'll make money from your real estate investments. Here are some common real estate investment strategies:

Rental Properties: This approach involves buying properties with the intention of renting them out to tenants for a long period of time. It's like becoming a landlord, where you earn regular rental income from the tenants. This strategy can provide a steady stream of cash flow and the potential for property value appreciation over time.

Fix-and-Flip: This strategy involves purchasing properties that are undervalued or in need of renovation. After fixing them up, you sell them for a higher price to make a profit. It's like buying a house, giving it a makeover, and then selling it for a higher price. This strategy requires knowledge of property value and renovation costs, as well as the ability to sell the property quickly.

Real Estate Investment Trusts (REITs): REITs are investment vehicles that allow you to invest in real estate without directly owning and managing properties. It's like investing in a company that owns and operates different real estate properties. By investing in publicly traded REITs, you can earn income from rental properties, commercial buildings, or other real estate assets. This strategy provides the benefits of real estate ownership while offering liquidity and diversification.

Development Projects: This strategy involves participating in property development projects, either on your own or as part of a joint venture with other investors. It's like being part of a team that builds new properties or develops existing ones. This strategy can be more complex and requires knowledge of construction, zoning regulations, and market demand. The potential for higher profits exists, but there are also higher risks involved.

Wholesaling: This strategy involves finding properties that are underpriced or distressed and then assigning the contract to another investor for a fee. It's like acting as a middleman, connecting sellers and buyers and earning a fee for facilitating the transaction. This strategy requires good networking skills and the ability to find good deals.

Syndication: Syndication involves pooling funds with other investors to acquire larger properties or projects that might be too expensive or risky to pursue individually. It's like forming a team with other investors to buy a big property together. This strategy allows you to access larger real estate opportunities and share the risks and rewards with other investors.

You see, each investment approach has its own characteristics, risks, and potential rewards. It's important to choose the strategy that aligns with your financial goals, resources, and risk tolerance.

Building a successful real estate investment strategy requires a combination of market knowledge, financial analysis, risk management, and continuous learning. When you follow these steps and remain disciplined, you can develop a strategy that aligns with your goals and positions you for long-term success in the real estate market.

Chapter 3

Understanding Property Ownership

Now, Kwame has got a property but renovating the property proved to be a challenging endeavor for him. The building required significant structural repairs, including electrical and plumbing upgrades. Unforeseen issues cropped up during the renovation process, testing Kwame's resilience and problem-solving skills.

However, Kwame remained undeterred. He enlisted the expertise of a reliable team of architects, contractors, and project managers who shared his vision for the building. They worked tirelessly to address the challenges, ensuring that the project stayed on track and within budget.

Kwame also focused on creating a sustainable and eco-friendly living space. He incorporated energy-efficient features, such as solar panels and water-saving fixtures, to reduce the building's environmental impact and attract environmentally conscious tenants.

Once the renovations were complete, Kwame turned his attention to effective property management. He understood that the success of his investment depended on maintaining the property's appeal and ensuring tenant satisfaction.

He also hired a skilled property manager who shared his commitment to exceptional service and building strong tenant relationships. Together, they developed strategies to attract high-quality tenants and create a sense of community within the building. They organized social events, implemented efficient maintenance processes, and actively listened to tenant feedback.

As the property flourished under Kwame's management, his reputation as a reliable and responsible landlord grew. Word spread within the real estate community, and he began receiving inquiries about potential joint ventures and investment opportunities. He also ensured to put structures into what he was doing.

What Kwame did was what we did with the Wisdom Kwati Smart City project. The goal was to provide efficient housing solutions and give residents and property owners the best of living experience. But before you jump into owning that property, you must get to know what is involved.

Navigating the legal and regulatory frameworks is a critical aspect of real estate investing in Nigeria and Africa. Understanding property ownership laws and regulations, working with real estate professionals and legal advisors, and managing documentation and permits are essential for a smooth and compliant investment process.

Property Ownership Laws and Regulations

If you're planning to buy a piece of land or a property in a certain country or region, before you make any decisions, it's really important to understand the laws and regulations that govern property ownership in that particular place. Just like different countries have different rules for driving or different sports have different sets of rules, each country or region has its own set of laws that determine how property ownership works.

These laws cover various aspects of property ownership, such as how land can be owned, how it can be transferred from one person to another, and how it can be used. Some of the important things these laws address include land tenure (how land can be held or owned), land registration (the process of officially recording ownership of land), property rights (the rights and protections that come with owning property), zoning regulations (rules that determine how land can be used in different areas), and building codes (rules that specify how structures can be built).

Let's take Nigeria as an example. In Nigeria, there is a law called the Land Use Act of 1978 that governs land ownership. According to this law, the government actually owns the land, but individuals and organizations can obtain a document called a Certificate of Occupancy. This certificate gives them legal rights to use the land for a specific purpose, like building a house or starting a business.

To make sure you're on the right side of the law and to avoid any legal problems, it's essential to become familiar with the specific laws and regulations that apply to the place where you want to invest. This may involve consulting with legal professionals or seeking guidance from local experts who are knowledgeable about the property ownership requirements and procedures in that particular jurisdiction. They can help you understand the specific steps you need to follow and the legal requirements you need to meet in order to ensure a smooth and lawful property ownership process.

Working with Real Estate Professionals and Legal Advisors

If you're about to embark on a complex journey, like exploring a dense forest, to navigate through it safely and make the best decisions, it's wise to have some experienced guides and experts by your side. Similarly, when it comes to dealing with real estate, it's highly recommended to work with professionals who specialize in this field and legal advisors who understand the intricacies of real estate law.

Real estate professionals, like agents, brokers, and property managers, are like skilled guides who have a deep understanding of the real estate market. They know the ins and outs of the industry and can help you find good investment opportunities. They have access to valuable market information and can assist you in conducting research and investigations to make sure you're making informed decisions. Just like a forest guide who knows the secret paths and hidden dangers of the forest, real estate professionals can guide you through the complex process of buying, selling, or managing properties.

Legal advisors, on the other hand, are like legal experts who act as your legal guides throughout your real estate journey. They specialize in real estate law, which means they have a deep understanding of the legal rules and regulations that govern property transactions. Think of them as your legal navigators who help you navigate the legal aspects of real estate. They can review contracts and agreements to ensure everything is in order and that your interests are protected. They guide you through the legal complexities and ensure you comply with all the necessary regulations.

In addition to reviewing documents, legal advisors can also provide valuable guidance on various legal matters related to real estate. They can explain the legal implications of different property transactions, help you negotiate favorable terms, and identify potential legal risks. Their expertise can help you avoid legal pitfalls and make sure your real estate ventures proceed smoothly and legally.

By working with real estate professionals and legal advisors, you benefit from their knowledge and expertise. They can help you make well-informed decisions, protect your interests, and navigate the complex legal and regulatory frameworks involved in real estate transactions. These professionals can make your real estate journey more efficient and less risky.

Managing Documentation, Permits, and Legal Requirements

Imagine you're planning to build a house or renovate your current one. There's a lot of paperwork involved in making your plans a reality, just like when you're preparing for a big event or party. You need to have invitations, contracts, permits, and other documents in order to ensure everything runs smoothly and legally.

In real estate, it's no different. When you're involved in buying, selling, or leasing property, there's a substantial amount of paperwork and legal requirements to take care of. This includes documents like sale agreements, lease agreements, property titles (which prove ownership), land surveys, building permits, and other important papers. It's crucial to make sure all these documents are properly prepared, reviewed, and executed to establish legal ownership and protect your investment.

Think of it as organizing a big event. You need to send out invitations (like sale or lease agreements) to the right people, and they need to respond and sign the agreements. You also need to make sure you have the proper permits for things like constructing a new building or making renovations. It's like getting the necessary permissions to set up decorations, play music, or serve food at your event.

Without these permits, you might face legal issues or even penalties.

To make sure everything is in order, it's important to work with legal advisors. They are like event planners who specialize in the legal aspects of real estate. They can help you with the necessary paperwork, such as conducting title searches and due diligence. It's like they investigate the background of the property to make sure everything is clear and there are no ownership disputes or debts attached to it.

Just as an event planner ensures you comply with the rules and regulations of the venue, legal advisors can guide you through the compliance with regulatory requirements in real estate. This includes obtaining the proper permits for construction or renovations, following zoning regulations (which determine how the property can be used), and adhering to environmental and safety standards. It's like ensuring your event venue meets all the safety codes and regulations, so everyone can enjoy the event without any problems.

When you familiarize yourself with the specific legal requirements and engaging experts who specialize in these areas, you can avoid potential delays or penalties. It's like having a team of experienced event planners who know all the ins and outs of organizing successful events. They can guide you through the process, make sure you have all the necessary documents, and ensure your real estate transactions are legally sound and compliant with the regulations.

So, just as proper planning and organization are essential for a successful event, managing documentation, permits, and legal requirements is crucial for smooth and legally sound real estate transactions. Legal advisors are your trusted event planners who help you navigate through the paperwork, obtain the necessary permits, and ensure your investment is protected.

Due Diligence and Risk Mitigation

Imagine you're interested in buying a used car. Before making a decision, you'd want to do some research and inspect the car to make sure it's in good condition and there are no hidden problems. You want to avoid buying a car that might break down soon or has legal issues, right?

In real estate, a similar process called due diligence is important before making an investment. Due diligence means thoroughly investigating and researching the property to identify any potential risks or problems. It's like doing a background check on the car, inspecting its condition, and making sure everything is in order.

During due diligence, you would want to dig into the history of the property. Just as you'd want to know the car's maintenance history and accident records, in real estate, you'd research the property's ownership history. You want to verify that the person selling the property is the rightful owner and that there are no legal disputes or claims against it.

Also, be involved in the process as much as you can. I once assigned a team member to do due diligence on a property we acquired and it turned out a loss for us. This would have been averted if I showed up to review the entire processes. This has taught me to be involved in the due diligence process.

Also, work with professionals. Just as you would inspect the car to check for any mechanical issues or hidden damages, in real estate, property inspections are conducted. Professionals are brought in to examine the property's condition, identify any structural problems, and assess if there are any potential liabilities or risks associated with it. This ensures that you're fully aware of any issues that might require costly repairs or hinder your investment goals.

Working with legal advisors and real estate professionals is like having experienced mechanics and car experts help you with the inspection. They can review the property documents, such as titles and contracts, to ensure everything is legitimate and in order. They also have the expertise to assess any legal risks related to the property or the transaction. Just as a car expert might identify hidden problems that you might have missed, legal advisors and real estate professionals can spot potential legal issues that could arise during the transaction and propose strategies to mitigate those risks.

The purpose of conducting due diligence is to make informed investment decisions. When you research and inspect the property, you can identify any red flags, legal complications, or financial risks. This allows you to avoid potential problems and make a well-informed choice that aligns with your investment goals.

In summary, due diligence in real estate is similar to researching and inspecting a used car before purchasing it. It involves investigating the property's history, verifying ownership, inspecting its condition, and assessing any potential risks or legal issues. Legal advisors and real estate professionals act as your experts, helping you navigate this process and ensuring that you're aware of any risks and have strategies in place to mitigate them.

Staying Updated on Legal Changes

Real estate regulations and laws can change over time. It is essential to stay updated on any changes in the legal and regulatory frameworks that may impact your investments. This includes monitoring changes in property ownership laws, taxation policies, land use regulations, and other relevant legislation. Staying informed allows you to adjust your investment strategy accordingly and ensure ongoing compliance with the evolving legal landscape.

Local Laws and Customs: In addition to national laws and regulations, it is crucial to consider local laws and customs that may vary within a country or region. Different areas may have specific regulations regarding property ownership, development, or land use. Understanding these local nuances is important to ensure compliance and avoid potential legal issues.

Land Titles and Registration: In many African countries, land ownership may be subject to complex and informal systems. It is important to conduct thorough research and due diligence to verify the validity of land titles and ensure proper registration. Engaging the services of professionals who are familiar with local land tenure systems can help navigate these complexities and provide insights into title verification processes.

Joint Ventures and Partnerships: Real estate investments in Nigeria and Africa often involve joint ventures or partnerships with local entities or individuals. It is essential to establish clear legal agreements and contracts that outline the roles, responsibilities, and ownership structure of each party. Working with legal advisors who are experienced in structuring joint venture agreements can help protect your interests and mitigate potential disputes.

Taxation and Financial Regulations: Real estate investments are subject to taxation, and the tax regulations can vary from country to country. It is crucial to understand the tax implications of your investments, including property taxes, capital gains taxes, and withholding taxes. Consulting with tax professionals who specialize in real estate can help optimize your tax planning and ensure compliance with financial regulations.

Compliance with Environmental and Building Regulations: Environmental regulations and building codes play a crucial role in real estate development. Ensure that your projects adhere to environmental protection standards and obtain the necessary permits and approvals. Non-compliance can lead to legal consequences, financial penalties, or project delays. Engaging environmental consultants and architects who are knowledgeable about local regulations can help navigate these requirements.

Dispute Resolution Mechanisms: Real estate investments may encounter disputes or conflicts. Understanding the available dispute resolution mechanisms, such as negotiation, mediation, or arbitration, is important for timely and cost-effective resolution. Consider including dispute resolution clauses in contracts and agreements to establish a framework for resolving disputes amicably.

Compliance with Anti-Corruption Laws: Corruption can be a challenge in some African countries. Ensure that your investment activities adhere to anti-corruption laws and ethical business practices. Engage in transparent transactions, conduct thorough due diligence on business partners, and implement robust internal controls to mitigate corruption risks.

Continuous Legal Support: Real estate investment is an ongoing process that requires continuous legal support. Engage legal advisors who specialize in real estate to provide guidance throughout your investment journey. They can assist with contract negotiations, lease agreements, property transfers, and other legal matters that may arise during property management or portfolio expansion.

Regular Legal Audits: Conduct regular legal audits to review the compliance of your real estate investments with applicable laws and regulations. This helps identify any potential legal risks or areas of non-compliance that need to be addressed. Periodic legal audits contribute to the long-term sustainability and success of your real estate portfolio.

Professional Associations and Industry Bodies: Joining professional associations and industry bodies related to real estate can provide valuable networking opportunities, access to resources, and updates on legal and regulatory developments. These organizations often offer educational programs, seminars, and conferences that can enhance your understanding of legal frameworks and industry best practices.

Building Relationships with Local Authorities: Developing positive relationships with local authorities, such as government agencies, regulatory bodies, and municipalities, can facilitate the smooth processing of permits and approvals. Building rapport and maintaining open lines of communication can help navigate bureaucratic processes and resolve any issues that may arise.

Local Legal Considerations: Each African country has its own legal system and nuances. It is important to familiarize yourself with the legal landscape of the specific country or region where you plan to invest. Engaging local legal advisors who are well-versed in the local laws and regulations can provide invaluable insights and guidance.

Intellectual Property Protection: In the real estate industry, intellectual property rights can play a role in protecting architectural designs, brand identities, and marketing materials. Understanding the intellectual property laws in the relevant jurisdiction and taking appropriate steps to protect your intellectual property assets can safeguard your investments and brand reputation.

Compliance with Anti-Money Laundering (AML) Regulations: Real estate transactions can be vulnerable to money laundering and illicit activities. To mitigate these risks, it is important to comply with AML regulations. Conduct due diligence on your business partners, clients, and sources of funding to ensure transparency and compliance with AML laws and regulations.

Legal Due Diligence on Property Transactions: Legal due diligence is a critical step in any real estate transaction. It involves a comprehensive review of property documents, contracts, leases, permits, and any potential legal issues or encumbrances. Legal advisors can assist in conducting due diligence to uncover any legal risks or liabilities associated with the property and ensure a smooth transfer of ownership.

Lease Agreements and Tenant Relations: If you plan to invest in rental properties, understanding and complying with tenancy laws and regulations is essential. Lease agreements should be carefully drafted to protect your interests as a landlord while also adhering to local laws regarding tenant rights, eviction procedures, and lease terms. Building positive tenant relations and addressing any legal issues promptly can contribute to the success of your rental properties.

Compliance with Data Protection Laws: With the increasing reliance on technology and digital platforms in real estate, it is important to be aware of data protection and privacy laws. Ensure that you handle and protect personal and sensitive data in accordance with applicable data protection regulations to maintain the trust and confidence of your clients and stakeholders.

Insurance Coverage: Adequate insurance coverage is crucial in mitigating risks associated with real estate investments. Consider obtaining appropriate insurance policies to protect your properties, assets, and liability exposures. Consult insurance professionals who specialize in real estate to assess the specific risks involved and determine the most suitable coverage for your investment portfolio.

Keeping Abreast of Regulatory Changes: Regulatory frameworks and laws governing real estate can evolve over time. Stay updated on any changes or amendments to existing laws and regulations that may impact your investments. Engaging with industry associations, attending seminars, and maintaining a network of professionals can help you stay informed about the latest legal developments and adapt your strategies accordingly.

In the next Chapter, we will look at how to diversify your portfolio.

Chapter 4

Diversifying the Portfolio

With the success of his first investment, Kwame felt empowered to expand his real estate portfolio. He continued to conduct thorough market research and identified emerging trends and untapped opportunities.

Kwame diversified his investments, acquiring properties in different sectors of the real estate market. He ventured into commercial spaces, including office buildings and retail centers, recognizing the growing demand for workspace and retail outlets in Nairobi's expanding economy. He also explored mixed-use developments, combining residential and commercial spaces to create vibrant, self-sustaining communities.

As Kwame's portfolio grew, so did his network of industry professionals and strategic partners. He collaborated with architects, interior designers, and landscape architects who shared his vision of creating sustainable, aesthetically pleasing spaces that enhanced the quality of life for residents and tenants.

Diversifying your real estate portfolio means spreading your investments across different types of properties or locations to reduce risk. Here are some simple explanations of various ways you can diversify your real estate holdings:

Residential Properties: These include houses, apartments, and condos where people live. They offer a steady rental income and are generally considered stable investments.

Commercial Properties: These are buildings used for business purposes, like offices, retail spaces, and warehouses. They can provide higher rental income, especially in prime locations.

Industrial Properties: These are properties like factories, warehouses, and distribution centers. They tend to have long-term leases and can be less sensitive to economic downturns.

Vacation Rentals: These are properties rented out to tourists or vacationers. They can provide higher short-term rental income, but they may also have higher management costs.

Real Estate Investment Trusts (REITs): REITs are like mutual funds for real estate. They pool money from multiple investors to invest in a diversified portfolio of properties. Investing in REITs offers exposure to real estate without directly owning properties.

Raw Land: This is undeveloped land that can be held for potential future development or appreciation. It doesn't generate rental income, but its value can increase over time.

Fix-and-Flip Properties: This involves buying properties at a lower price, renovating or improving them, and then selling them at a higher price. It's a more active form of real estate investing.

Real Estate Crowdfunding: This involves multiple investors pooling their resources to invest in larger real estate projects. It allows individuals to participate in bigger deals with a smaller investment.

Real Estate Partnerships or Syndications: This is when multiple investors come together to collectively invest in a property. Each investor contributes capital, and profits and risks are shared.

International Real Estate: Investing in real estate in other countries can provide exposure to different markets and potentially higher returns. However, it comes with additional challenges and risks.

Mixed-Use Properties: These properties combine different types, like residential units with retail spaces. They can provide multiple income streams and reduce dependency on a single market segment.

Real Estate Development: This involves buying land, obtaining necessary permits, and constructing buildings or developments. It can be a higher-risk, higher-reward strategy.

Each type of real estate investment has its own benefits and risks. It's important to do thorough research, consider your risk tolerance, and possibly consult with professionals or advisors before making any significant investments.

Chapter 5

Financing Your Real Estate Investment

A lot of people like Kwame want to begin their real estate investment journey but do not understand the part of Financing. Financing is a crucial aspect of real estate investing, and understanding the available options in Nigeria and Africa is essential for successful investment ventures.

Now, let's discuss various financing options, including mortgage options, working with financial institutions, evaluating alternative funding sources, and exploring investment partnerships.

Traditional Financing Options

Let's imagine you want to buy a house or invest in real estate in Nigeria or Africa, but you don't have all the money you need upfront. In this case, traditional financing options can help you. Think of traditional financing options as going to a bank to borrow money for your real estate investment. Just like when you borrow money from a friend, the bank lends you the money you need, and you agree to pay it back over time. However, there are some important things to consider.

First, the bank wants to make sure that you're trustworthy and capable of paying back the loan. It's like when your friend wants to lend you money but wants to know if you'll be able to pay them back. The bank will assess your creditworthiness, which means they'll look at your financial history, like your income, expenses, and whether you've paid back loans in the past. They want to be sure you have a good track record of managing your money responsibly.

Second, the bank may ask for something valuable as collateral. Collateral is like a guarantee or security for the bank in case you're unable to repay the loan. It's similar to when your friend asks you to leave something valuable with them as a guarantee that you'll return their money. If you can't repay the loan, the bank may take possession of the collateral to recover the money they lent you.

Finally, the bank charges you extra money for lending you the funds. This extra money is called interest, and it's a percentage of the loan amount that you have to pay back along with the principal (the original amount borrowed). It's like when your friend lends you money, but they also want you to give them a little bit extra as a thank-you for borrowing their money.

To secure traditional financing, it's important to have a good credit history, which shows that you're responsible with your finances. You should also have financial stability, meaning you have a stable income and can afford to make the loan payments. Additionally, having a solid business plan, especially if you're investing in real estate for profit, helps convince the bank that you have a well-thought-out strategy to make the investment successful.

Remember, traditional financing options from banks and financial institutions can be a helpful way to obtain the funds you need for real estate investments, but it's important to understand the requirements, such as creditworthiness, collateral, and paying interest, to ensure you can secure the financing successfully.

Mortgage Options

Imagine you want to buy a house, but you don't have enough money to pay for it all at once. That's where a mortgage comes in. A mortgage is like a special kind of loan that you can get from a bank or a financial institution to help you buy the house. It's like asking someone to lend you the money to buy the house, and you agree to pay them back over time, with some extra money added as interest for the favor they're doing for you.

Now, there are different types of mortgages available to you, and they work a bit differently:

Fixed-rate mortgage: This is like signing up for a fixed-price subscription plan. You agree that no matter what happens to interest rates in the future, your monthly mortgage payments will always stay the same. It's like knowing exactly how much you'll pay every month, just like when you subscribe to a streaming service and pay the same amount every month regardless of price changes.

Adjustable-rate mortgage: This one is a bit different. It's like getting a mortgage with a flexible interest rate that can change over time, like a variable price for something you buy regularly. The interest rate may go up or down depending on the economy or other factors, so your monthly payments can change too. It's a bit riskier because you may end up paying more if the interest rates go up, but you could also benefit if they go down.

Government-backed mortgage: This is like having the government step in to help you get a mortgage. It's like having a special guarantee from the government that makes the bank more willing to lend you the money at better terms. It's similar to having a co-signer when you borrow money from someone, making the bank more confident that you'll pay it back.

In Nigeria, for example, the Federal Mortgage Bank provides government-backed mortgages, making it easier and more affordable for certain eligible people to buy a house.

To make the best decision for your situation, you need to understand these different mortgage options available in your country. Compare things like interest rates (the extra money you pay back to the lender), the terms (how long you have to pay back the loan), and the eligibility criteria (the requirements you need to meet to qualify for a mortgage).

By doing so, you can make an informed choice about the best mortgage for your needs and financial situation, just like you would compare different phone plans or subscription services to find the one that suits you best.

Financial Institutions

Think of financial institutions as big stores that offer a wide range of financial products and services. These stores can be banks, credit unions, or microfinance institutions. Just like you go to a regular store to buy different things, you go to financial institutions to access various financial tools and services.

Now, let's look at some of the services they offer:

Mortgage loans: A mortgage loan is like a special type of loan that you can get from a financial institution to buy a house. It's similar to going to a store and asking for a loan specifically to purchase something big, like a car or a computer. The financial institution lends you the money, and you agree to pay it back over time, usually with some extra money added as interest.

Bridge loans: Imagine you want to buy a new house before selling your current one. You need some money to make that happen, right? A bridge loan is like a temporary loan from a financial institution that helps you "bridge" the gap between buying your new house and selling your old one.

It's like borrowing money to cover the cost of the new house until you can pay it back when you sell your current house.

Construction loans: If you're planning to build a house from scratch, a construction loan is like a financial tool that helps you fund the building process. It's like having a specific loan designed to pay for all the materials, labor, and other expenses involved in constructing your house.

Portfolio financing: This is like having a financial institution help you manage and finance multiple real estate investments. It's like having a personal financial advisor who assists you in organizing and funding your various real estate ventures. They can help you with the financial aspects of buying, selling, or refinancing multiple properties.

To make the most of your relationship with financial institutions, it's important to build a good rapport with them, just like you would with a store owner or a shopkeeper. Show them that you're financially stable, meaning you have a good track record of managing your money and paying back loans. Additionally, present a well-structured investment plan, which is like having a clear roadmap for your real estate investments, demonstrating that you've thought through your strategy and potential returns.

By doing these things, you increase your chances of getting favorable terms when seeking financing from financial institutions, making it easier and more affordable to access the financial products and services they offer.

Alternative Funding Sources

When it comes to getting money for real estate investments, traditional options like banks might not always be available or suitable for everyone. That's where alternative funding sources come in. They are like different stores or platforms where you can find money for your real estate projects when the usual options are limited.

Here are some examples of alternative funding sources:

Private lenders (hard money lenders): Think of private lenders as specialized stores that offer short-term loans for real estate projects. They are different from traditional banks because they have higher interest rates and are more flexible with their requirements. It's like going to a local shop where the owner is willing to lend you money quickly, but they might charge you a bit more interest than a big bank would. The loans from private lenders are usually for a shorter period, so you need to pay them back relatively quickly.

Real estate investment trusts (REITs): REITs are like investment clubs or groups where people pool their money together to invest in different real estate projects. It's similar to joining a club where each member contributes some money, and then the club uses that money to buy different properties. By investing in a REIT, you become a part-owner of a diverse portfolio of real estate properties. It's like being part of a group that collectively owns multiple stores or buildings.

Crowdfunding platforms: Crowdfunding platforms are like online marketplaces where people can invest in real estate projects collectively. It's like a virtual marketplace where individuals come together to support and invest in different real estate ventures. Imagine a platform where you can contribute a small amount of money, and when many people do the same, it adds up to fund a real estate project. It's like a crowdfunding campaign where people contribute small amounts to support a cause, but instead of a cause, it's a real estate project.

Angel investors: Angel investors are like individuals or groups who believe in your real estate project and provide money in exchange for a share in the project's ownership. It's like finding someone who is willing to invest in your idea and become a partner in your business. They provide capital, which is like the funds you need for your project, and in return, they get a stake in the project's success.

Before you proceed with any of these alternative funding sources, it's important to evaluate the terms, risks, and potential returns associated with each option. It's like carefully examining the offerings, policies, and potential benefits of different stores or platforms before deciding where to spend your money. By understanding the details, you can make informed decisions about which alternative funding source is the best fit for your real estate project.

Investment Partnerships

If you have a big project that requires a lot of money and expertise, like starting a business or building a large structure, but you don't have all the resources or knowledge to do it alone, that's where investment partnerships come in. It's like teaming up with other people or companies to pool your resources and skills together to achieve a common goal.

Here are a couple of examples of investment partnerships:

Joint ventures: A joint venture is like forming a team with other people or companies to work on a specific project together. It's similar to a group of friends coming together to organize a big event. Each person contributes something valuable, like money, skills, or connections, and everyone shares in the risks and rewards of the project. It's a collaborative effort where all parties have a say in the decision-making process and share in the profits or losses that result from the venture.

Limited partnerships: In a limited partnership, there are two types of roles: active investors and passive investors. It's like having a business where one person takes charge of all the day-to-day operations, making important decisions and running the show (active investor), while others contribute money or resources but have a more hands-off role (passive investors). It's like having a business where you have a partner who manages everything on the ground, while you provide the financial support and have a share in the profits.

When considering investment partnerships, it's crucial to establish clear agreements and understandings among all parties involved. Think of it as creating a contract or a set of rules that outline the roles, responsibilities, expectations, and contributions of each partner. It's like setting the ground rules and expectations for everyone involved in the partnership, just like you would establish the terms and conditions for participating in a group project or organizing a team event.

It's also important to define how the profits and losses will be distributed among the partners. This is similar to deciding how the financial benefits or costs will be divided among the team members after a successful event. Additionally, decision-making processes should be outlined, clarifying how important choices will be made collectively or by specific individuals.

Engaging legal advisors is like seeking guidance from experts who specialize in partnership agreements. They can help structure the partnership in a way that protects the interests of all parties involved, ensuring that everyone's rights and responsibilities are clearly defined and legally protected.

By forming investment partnerships and establishing clear agreements, you can leverage additional capital and expertise, increasing your chances of success in your real estate or business ventures. It's like having a strong and capable team that combines different strengths and resources to achieve common goals.

Self-Financing

Imagine you have a goal to start a small business, like opening a bakery. You have two options to get the money you need: either borrow it from someone else, like a bank, or use your own savings or the value of something you already own.

Self-financing is like using your own savings or the equity from existing properties to fund your real estate investments. It's similar to using your own money from your piggy bank or a jar where you've been saving up, or using the value of something you already own, like a valuable collection or an old car you don't use anymore.

Here are a couple of key points about self-financing:

Personal savings: If you have been setting aside money from your income or saving up over time, self-financing allows you to use those savings to invest in real estate. It's like using the money you've been putting away for a special occasion or a big purchase to fund your real estate ventures.

Equity from existing properties: Let's say you already own a house or a property that has increased in value over time. Self-financing allows you to tap into that value by taking out a loan against the property or selling it to raise funds for your new real estate investments. It's like using the value of something you already own, such as selling a valuable painting to finance your bakery.

The advantage of self-financing is that it gives you more control over your investment. You don't have to rely on external lenders, like banks, and you don't have to pay interest on a loan. It's like being your own boss and not having to answer to anyone else for the money you're using.

However, it's important to consider a few things:

Personal liquidity: Self-financing involves using your own money, which means tying up a portion of your funds in real estate investments. This may impact your personal liquidity, which is the amount of cash or easily accessible money you have available for other needs or emergencies. It's like having most of your money tied up in your bakery, making it less available for other purposes.

Opportunity cost: When you invest your own money in real estate, you should also consider the opportunity cost. This means considering what else you could do with that money if you didn't use it for real estate investments. For example, you could invest it in other businesses, save it for retirement, or use it for other personal goals. It's like thinking about the alternative uses or benefits of the money you're investing in your bakery.

When you self-finance, you have the advantage of using your own funds and having more control over your investments. However, it's essential to carefully assess your personal financial situation, the impact on your liquidity, and the potential opportunity cost before deciding to invest your own money in real estate.

Creative Financing Strategies

In addition to the above options, exploring creative financing strategies can help fund real estate investments. These strategies may include seller financing, lease options, seller carryback mortgages, or using retirement funds through self-directed IRAs. These strategies involve negotiating with sellers or property owners to structure financing arrangements that suit both parties. For example, seller financing allows the buyer to make payments directly to the seller, often with a predetermined interest rate and repayment schedule.

Lease options enable investors to lease a property with the option to buy it at a later date, providing flexibility and time to secure traditional financing. Seller carryback mortgages involve the seller providing a portion of the financing, acting as the lender for a portion of the purchase price. Self-directed IRAs allow individuals to use their retirement funds to invest in real estate, offering tax advantages and potential returns.

When evaluating financing options, it is important to consider the following:

a. Risk and Return: Assess the risk associated with each financing option and determine the potential returns. Evaluate interest rates, repayment terms, fees, and the impact on your overall investment returns. Consider the impact on cash flow, profitability, and the ability to achieve your investment objectives.

b. Eligibility Criteria: Understand the requirements and eligibility criteria for each financing option. This includes factors such as creditworthiness, income stability, collateral, and the specific qualifications imposed by lenders or investors. Determine whether you meet the criteria and if any additional steps or documentation are needed.

c. Financial Planning: Conduct a thorough analysis of your financial capacity and cash flow projections. Determine the amount of financing needed and assess your ability to service the debt or fulfill the financial obligations associated with the chosen financing option. Consider the impact on your personal finances and long-term financial goals.

d. Professional Advice: Seek advice from financial advisors, mortgage brokers, or real estate professionals who specialize in real estate financing. They can provide guidance on the available options, help evaluate the suitability of each option to your specific investment goals, and assist in navigating the application and approval processes.

e. Due Diligence: Conduct comprehensive due diligence on potential lenders, investors, or partners. Evaluate their reputation, track record, and reliability. Review the terms and conditions of financing agreements, including any potential risks, obligations, or contingencies. Engaging legal advisors can help ensure that the documentation and agreements are legally sound and protect your interests.

f. Exit Strategy: Consider your exit strategy in case you need to refinance, sell the property, or repay the financing. Evaluate the potential impact on your investment portfolio and determine the best approach to manage the financing arrangement throughout the investment lifecycle.

In conclusion, financing is a critical component of real estate investing in Nigeria and Africa. Exploring various financing options, understanding mortgage options, working with financial institutions, evaluating alternative funding sources, and exploring investment partnerships are key considerations for successfully financing your real estate investments.

When you access your financial capacity, conducting thorough research, seeking professional advice, and structuring financing arrangements that align with your investment objectives, you can effectively fund your real estate ventures and maximize your chances of success.

Chapter 6

Property Selection

As Kwame continued to succeed in the real estate industry, he became increasingly aware of the social responsibility that came with his accomplishments. He recognized the immense impact real estate could have on communities and vowed to use his resources and influence to make a positive difference.

Kwame initiated community development projects in underserved areas, working closely with local leaders and organizations. He focused on providing affordable housing options for low-income families, investing in the construction of apartment complexes and housing cooperatives. Kwame ensured that these developments included essential amenities such as schools, healthcare facilities, and recreational spaces.

Additionally, Kwame collaborated with nonprofit organizations to create vocational training programs that equipped community members with skills in construction, property management, and maintenance. He believed that empowering individuals with these skills would not only contribute to their personal growth but also stimulate economic development within the community.

Furthermore, Kwame was committed to environmental sustainability. He implemented green building practices, incorporating renewable energy sources, rainwater harvesting systems, and eco-friendly construction materials into his projects. By setting an example of sustainable development, he aimed to inspire others in the industry to prioritize environmental stewardship.

He was invited to speak to a group of young people who desired to go into Real Estate and a young man asked him, "How do I know the best properties to invest in and build my business around?" He was quiet for a few minutes before he went on to answer the question.

Property selection and due diligence are crucial steps in real estate investing. They involve identifying potential properties, conducting thorough inspections, and evaluating market trends and growth potential. To identify suitable investment properties, consider the following factors:

a. **Location**: Location is a fundamental factor that affects property value and potential returns. Look for properties in desirable areas with amenities, good infrastructure, access to transportation, and proximity to schools, hospitals, shopping centers, and employment hubs. Consider the neighborhood's reputation, safety, and future development plans.

b. **Market Demand**: Assess the demand for properties in the area. Research the rental market and vacancy rates if you plan to invest in rental properties. For commercial properties, evaluate the demand from businesses and potential tenants. Analyze population growth, employment opportunities, and economic indicators to gauge the overall market demand.

c. **Property Type**: Determine the property type that aligns with your investment goals. Options may include residential properties (apartments, houses), commercial properties (office buildings, retail spaces), industrial properties (warehouses, factories), or land for development. Consider the potential rental income, capital appreciation, and maintenance costs associated with each property type.

d. **Investment Strategy**: Clarify your investment strategy, whether it involves buying and holding properties for long-term appreciation, flipping properties for short-term gains, or developing properties for resale or rental income. This will help narrow down your property search and align with your investment objectives.

e. **Financing Considerations**: Evaluate the financial feasibility of the properties. Determine if the property aligns with your budget, financing options, and projected cash flow. Consider factors such as down payment requirements, mortgage options, property taxes, insurance, and maintenance costs. Conduct a financial analysis to estimate potential returns and assess the investment's viability.

Property Inspections and Due Diligence

Performing comprehensive due diligence is essential to uncover potential risks, assess the property's condition, and verify crucial details. Here are some key aspects to consider:

a. **Physical Inspection**: Inspect the property thoroughly, both inside and outside. Assess the structure, foundation, roofing, plumbing, electrical systems, and overall condition. Identify any existing or potential issues, such as water damage, pest infestations, mold, or structural defects. Engage professionals, such as home inspectors, architects, or engineers, to provide detailed assessments.

b. **Legal and Title Investigation**: Verify the property's legal status and ownership. Review the title documents, survey plans, and any existing encumbrances, liens, or disputes. Engage legal professionals to conduct a title search, ensuring that the property has a clear title and can be legally transferred. Verify compliance with local building codes, zoning regulations, and permits.

c. **Financial Analysis**: Evaluate the property's financials, including rental income potential, expenses, and projected cash flow. Analyze historical and projected operating expenses, such as property taxes, insurance, maintenance, and property management fees. Assess the rental market and rental rates to estimate potential income. Consider factors such as vacancy rates, tenant turnover, and potential rental growth.

d. **Market Analysis**: Evaluate market trends and dynamics in the area. Research recent property sales, rental rates, and market appreciation. Analyze economic indicators, population growth, job market stability, and future development plans. Consider factors that may affect property values and growth potential in the short and long term.

e. **Environmental Considerations**: Assess any environmental risks associated with the property, such as contamination or proximity to hazardous areas. Consider engaging environmental consultants to conduct assessments and provide reports on potential risks.

Property Valuation and Growth Potential

Determining the property's value and growth potential is crucial for investment decision-making. Imagine you are thinking about buying a house or a piece of land to make some money in the future. Before you make that decision, it's essential to understand two important things about the property: its value and its potential to grow in value over time. To achieve this, consider the following:

a. **Property Valuation**: Evaluate the property's value through various methods, such as the market approach, income approach, and cost approach. The market approach involves comparing the property to similar properties that have recently sold in the area. The income approach involves assessing the property's income potential and determining its value based on the expected cash flow. The cost approach estimates the property's value based on the cost of replacing or reproducing it.

b. **Rental Income Potential**: Assess the property's rental income potential if it is intended for rental purposes. Research rental rates in the area and evaluate the property's attractiveness to tenants. Consider factors such as location, amenities, size, and condition that may impact rental income.

c. **Capital Appreciation**: Consider the property's potential for capital appreciation over time. Evaluate historical price trends in the area and market indicators that suggest future growth. Assess factors such as infrastructure development, economic growth, population growth, and demand-supply dynamics that may influence property values positively.

d. **Exit Strategy**: Determine your exit strategy for the investment. Consider how you plan to monetize the property in the future, whether through resale, refinancing, or holding it long-term for rental income. Evaluate the potential returns and liquidity associated with each exit strategy.

e. **Professional Assistance**: Engage professionals such as real estate agents, appraisers, property managers, and market analysts to gain insights and expert advice. They can provide market data, property valuations, rental market analysis, and guidance on growth potential. Their expertise and local market knowledge can help you make informed decisions.

f. **Risk Assessment**: Identify and evaluate potential risks associated with the property and the investment. This includes assessing factors such as market volatility, economic instability, regulatory changes, environmental risks, and unforeseen expenses. Conduct a risk analysis to determine the level of risk tolerance and mitigate potential risks through proper risk management strategies.

In summary, property selection and due diligence are critical steps in real estate investing. By identifying potential properties, conducting thorough inspections, evaluating market trends, property valuation, and growth potential, you can make informed investment decisions.

Comprehensive due diligence minimizes risks, ensures you are investing in properties with potential for appreciation or income generation, and aligns with your investment objectives and strategy. Working with professionals, engaging in meticulous research, and conducting thorough assessments contribute to successful property selection and building a profitable real estate portfolio in Nigeria and Africa.

Chapter 7

Negotiation And Acquisition

Kwame's passion for real estate extended beyond his own ventures. He recognized the importance of sharing his knowledge and experiences to inspire and empower aspiring real estate entrepreneurs. Thus, he founded an organization dedicated to providing guidance, resources, and mentorship to young individuals interested in building their real estate fortunes.

Through the organization, Kwame conducted workshops, seminars, and online courses covering various aspects of real estate, from property acquisition and financing to property management and sustainable development. He invited industry experts and successful professionals to share their insights and experiences, creating a vibrant learning community.

Kwame also established mentorship programs within the organisation, pairing aspiring entrepreneurs with seasoned professionals in the real estate field. The mentorship relationships fostered personal and professional growth, offering guidance, support, and access to valuable networks.

By sharing his knowledge and providing a platform for others to learn and grow, Kwame aimed to create a ripple effect of positive change within the African real estate industry. He encouraged collaboration, networking, and ethical business practices, believing that collectively, they could elevate the industry and contribute to the continent's overall development. He also acknowledged how his negotiations skills helped him hit bigger deals in his investment journey.

Negotiation and acquisition strategies play a crucial role in real estate investment as they determine the terms, price, and overall success of acquiring a property. Developing effective negotiation skills, understanding local negotiation tactics and strategies, and managing the acquisition process are essential for investors.

Developing Negotiation Skills

Successful negotiation requires the development of key skills that enable you to communicate effectively, build rapport, and reach mutually beneficial agreements. Imagine you and a friend want to decide where to go for dinner, but you both have different preferences. Negotiation skills are like tools that can help you work together and find a solution that makes both of you happy. Some essential negotiation skills include:

a. Active Listening: Actively listen to the other party's needs, concerns, and objectives. Understanding their perspective allows you to identify potential areas of agreement and create win-win solutions.

b. Communication: Clearly articulate your goals, requirements, and expectations. Effective communication helps establish trust and ensures that both parties understand each other's positions.

c. Problem-Solving: Approach negotiations with a problem-solving mindset. Focus on finding creative solutions that address both parties' interests and maximize value.

d. Flexibility and Adaptability: Be open to alternative solutions and be willing to compromise when appropriate. Flexibility allows for greater negotiation opportunities and can lead to successful outcomes.

e. Emotional Intelligence: Understand and manage emotions during negotiations. Emotional intelligence helps you stay composed, empathize with the other party, and find common ground.

Negotiation Tactics and Strategies

Imagine you're at a flea market trying to buy a vintage item. Each flea market may have its own specific rules and ways of bargaining, and it's important to understand these dynamics to negotiate successfully. Here are some common negotiation tactics that can help you get a better deal:

a. Establishing Rapport: When you're negotiating, it's important to build a positive relationship with the seller. It's like making small talk and finding common ground with the seller, such as sharing your love for vintage items or showing respect and professionalism. This friendly approach creates a more cooperative atmosphere, increasing the chances of reaching an agreement.

b. Gathering Information: Before you start bargaining, gather as much information as you can. It's like doing research on the item you want to buy, understanding its value, and learning about market conditions. Additionally, try to find out the seller's motivations and constraints. This knowledge gives you an advantage during negotiations because you can use it to your benefit.

c. Setting Limits and Walk-Away Points: Determine your limits and non-negotiable terms in advance. It's like deciding the maximum price you're willing to pay for the vintage item or the minimum conditions it should meet. This helps you maintain control during negotiations and ensures that you don't agree to unfavorable terms. If the seller doesn't meet your walk-away points, you're prepared to walk away from the deal.

d. Offering and Seeking Concessions: During negotiations, you can offer concessions strategically to create value and build goodwill. It's like offering to buy multiple items from the seller to get a discounted price or agreeing to pay in cash for a better deal. On the other hand, you can seek concessions from the seller as well, such as asking for a lower price or additional items included in the purchase. These give-and-take actions can help reach a mutually beneficial agreement.

e. Leveraging Market Conditions: Understand the current market conditions and trends to your advantage. It's like knowing whether the demand for vintage items is high or low at the flea market. If it's a buyer's market where there are more sellers than buyers, you have more negotiation power because the sellers want to make a sale. However, in a seller's market where there are more buyers than sellers, you may need to be more flexible in your negotiations.

When you employ these negotiation tactics, you can increase your chances of getting a better deal in the flea market. Similarly, in real estate or other negotiations, understanding the local context, building rapport, gathering information, setting limits, offering and seeking concessions strategically, and leveraging market conditions can help you navigate negotiations successfully and achieve favorable outcomes.

Structuring Deals and Managing the Acquisition Process

Once negotiations are successful, it's important to structure the deal appropriately and manage the acquisition process effectively. Consider the following:

a. Deal Structure: Determine the most suitable deal structure based on your investment objectives, financing options, and risk tolerance. This may involve cash purchases, mortgage financing, joint ventures, or other creative financing arrangements.

b. Legal Assistance: Engage legal professionals to draft and review contracts, purchase agreements, and other relevant documents. They can ensure that the deal is legally binding, protect your interests, and address any regulatory or compliance requirements.

c. Due Diligence: Continue the due diligence process by verifying property information, conducting inspections, and reviewing documentation to ensure all terms and conditions are met. This helps mitigate risks and ensures that the property meets your expectations.

d. Financing and Funding: Secure the necessary financing or funds to complete the acquisition. Work with financial institutions or explore alternative funding sources, such as private lenders or investment partnerships.

e. Timelines and Deadlines: Establish clear timelines and deadlines for various stages of the acquisition process. This helps ensure smooth progress and allows for necessary contingencies.

f. Professional Guidance: Seek guidance from experienced professionals, such as real estate agents, brokers, or consultants, who can provide insights and advice throughout the acquisition process. Their expertise can help you navigate challenges and make informed decisions.

By developing negotiation skills, understanding local negotiation tactics and strategies, and effectively managing the acquisition process, real estate investors can increase their chances of securing favorable deals and maximizing their investment returns.

Effective negotiation skills are essential for achieving successful property acquisitions. You should focus on building strong communication and problem-solving abilities. Active listening allows you to understand the needs and concerns of the other party, enabling you to find mutually beneficial solutions. Clear and assertive communication ensures that your own objectives and expectations are properly conveyed.

Understanding local negotiation tactics and strategies is crucial, as these can vary across different regions and cultures. In some contexts, building rapport and establishing a positive relationship with the other party may be critical to successful negotiations. Gathering as much information as possible about the property, market conditions, and the motivations of the other party provides a competitive advantage. Setting limits and walk-away points in advance helps you as an investor maintain control during negotiations and avoid making unfavorable concessions.

Structuring the deal appropriately is another important aspect of the acquisition process. You need to consider their investment goals, financing options, and risk tolerance when deciding on the deal structure. Engaging legal professionals is crucial to ensure that all necessary contracts and agreements are properly drafted and reviewed. They can also assist in addressing any legal or regulatory requirements associated with the acquisition.

Continuing the due diligence process is crucial even after negotiations have concluded. This involves verifying property information, conducting inspections, and reviewing documentation to ensure that the property meets expectations and is free from any undisclosed issues or risks. Obtaining financing or securing funds to complete the acquisition is another critical step. You should explore various financing options, such as mortgage loans or partnerships, and ensure that you have the necessary funds available to close the deal.

Establishing clear timelines and deadlines for different stages of the acquisition process is important for efficient management. This helps ensure that tasks are completed on time and that any necessary contingencies can be addressed.

Seeking professional guidance from experienced real estate agents, brokers, or consultants can provide valuable insights and expertise throughout the acquisition process. Their knowledge of the local market and industry can help investors navigate challenges, make informed decisions, and optimize their investment strategy.

In conclusion, negotiation and acquisition strategies are integral to successful real estate investing. When you develop effective negotiation skills, understanding local tactics and strategies, and managing the acquisition process with thoroughness and professionalism can greatly enhance your ability to secure favorable deals and achieve your investment objectives.

Chapter 8

Property Management

As years passed, Kwame's real estate empire continued to expand, leaving an indelible mark on the African landscape. His dedication to community development, sustainable practices, and mentorship had transformed neighborhoods, uplifted lives, and inspired a new generation of real estate entrepreneurs.

Kwame's success was not measured solely by financial gains. His true fulfillment came from witnessing the transformative impact his projects had on individuals and communities. He received numerous accolades and recognition for his contributions, but his greatest reward was seeing families thrive in safe, affordable homes, witnessing small businesses flourish in his commercial spaces, and observing the ripple effect of empowerment.

As Kwame looked back on his journey, he knew that his mission was far from over. He remained committed to leaving a lasting legacy of positive change. He continued to innovate, adapt to emerging market trends, and explore new avenues within the real estate industry.

Kwame also dedicated a significant portion of his resources to philanthropic endeavors. He established scholarship programs to support underprivileged students pursuing careers in real estate, and he contributed to initiatives that addressed social and environmental challenges in African communities.

In doing so, Kwame ensured that his impact extended beyond his lifetime, fostering a legacy of prosperity, empowerment, and sustainable development in the African real estate landscape. He also ensured an effective property management system for his business.

Effective property management is crucial for real estate investors to ensure the smooth operation, maintenance, and profitability of their properties. It involves establishing property management systems and processes, managing tenants, handling maintenance and repairs, and optimizing rental income and property performance. Let's explore each of these aspects in detail:

Property Management Systems

To effectively manage a property, you need to establish robust systems and processes that streamline operations. This includes:

a. Tenant Screening and Selection: Implement a thorough tenant screening process to ensure reliable and responsible tenants. This may involve background checks, credit assessments, employment verification, and rental history verification. Selecting quality tenants reduces the risk of rent defaults and property damage.

b. Lease Agreements and Documentation: Develop comprehensive lease agreements that clearly outline tenant responsibilities, rental terms, and property rules. Maintain accurate documentation of lease agreements, tenant communications, and financial records for legal and accounting purposes.

c. Financial Management: Set up systems to manage rent collection, expense tracking, and accounting. Use software or property management tools to streamline rent payments, generate financial reports, and monitor cash flow. Regularly review expenses, budgets, and rental rates to optimize profitability.

d. Communication and Tenant Relations: Establish clear communication channels with tenants to address their concerns, handle inquiries, and ensure a positive tenant experience. Promptly respond to maintenance requests and maintain open lines of communication to foster good landlord-tenant relationships.

Dealing with Tenants, Maintenance, and Repairs

Managing tenants, maintenance, and repairs is an ongoing responsibility that requires prompt attention and efficient handling. Consider the following:

a. Maintenance and Repairs: Implement a proactive maintenance strategy to preserve the property's condition and address issues promptly. Regularly inspect the property, perform preventive maintenance tasks, and promptly respond to repair requests. Build relationships with reliable contractors and vendors to ensure quality and timely repairs.

b. Tenant Retention and Satisfaction: Maintain positive tenant relationships by addressing their concerns promptly, providing exceptional customer service, and being responsive to their needs. Proactive communication and addressing maintenance issues quickly can contribute to higher tenant satisfaction and longer tenancies.

c. Lease Renewals and Vacancies: Plan for lease renewals in advance to minimize vacancies. Evaluate market rental rates and consider offering incentives to encourage lease renewals. When a property becomes vacant, promptly market it, conduct tenant screenings, and efficiently complete the turnover process to minimize rental income loss.

Maximizing Rental Income and Optimizing Property Performance

To maximize rental income and optimize property performance, you should focus on:

a. Rental Market Analysis: Regularly assess rental market conditions to determine optimal rental rates. Research comparable properties in the area and consider factors such as demand, location, property features, and market trends. Adjust rental rates accordingly to remain competitive and attract quality tenants.

b. Property Upgrades and Amenities: Evaluate opportunities to enhance the property's value and attract tenants. Consider cost-effective upgrades, such as fresh paint, landscaping improvements, or adding desirable amenities like laundry facilities, parking spaces, or fitness centers. These enhancements can justify higher rental rates and increase tenant satisfaction.

c. Expense Management: Monitor and control expenses to optimize property performance. Analyze operating costs, such as utilities, insurance, maintenance, and property management fees, and identify areas for potential savings or cost reductions. Regularly review vendor contracts and seek competitive bids to ensure cost-effectiveness.

d. Performance Tracking and Reporting: Implement systems to track key performance indicators (KPIs) such as occupancy rates, rental income, tenant turnover, and maintenance costs. Regularly analyze these metrics to identify trends, assess property performance, and make data-driven decisions to improve profitability.

When you implement effective property management systems, handle tenant-related matters efficiently, and optimize rental income and property performance, you can ensure the long-term success of your real estate investments. Effective property management involves establishing systems and processes that streamline operations, ensuring tenant satisfaction, managing maintenance and repairs, and maximizing rental income and property performance.

Establishing property management systems and processes provides structure and consistency in managing properties. This includes implementing tenant screening procedures to select reliable tenants, creating comprehensive lease agreements that outline tenant responsibilities, and maintaining accurate documentation for legal and accounting purposes. Additionally, using software or property management tools can help streamline financial management, rent collection, and reporting processes.

Dealing with tenants, maintenance, and repairs requires prompt and efficient handling. Property managers should prioritize proactive maintenance to preserve the property's condition and promptly address repair requests. Building relationships with reliable contractors and vendors ensures timely and quality repairs.

Effective communication with tenants is crucial for addressing their concerns, maintaining good landlord-tenant relationships, and promoting tenant satisfaction. By promptly addressing maintenance issues and providing exceptional customer service, property managers can enhance tenant satisfaction and increase tenant retention.

Maximizing rental income and optimizing property performance involves several strategies. Regular rental market analysis helps determine competitive rental rates based on factors such as location, property features, and market demand.

Property upgrades and amenities can attract tenants and justify higher rental rates. By continuously evaluating operating costs and seeking cost-effective solutions, property managers can control expenses and improve profitability. Tracking key performance indicators such as occupancy rates, rental income, and maintenance costs allows for data-driven decision-making and the identification of areas for improvement.

Furthermore, property managers should proactively plan for lease renewals to minimize vacancies and ensure consistent rental income. When a property becomes vacant, efficient marketing and tenant screening processes help reduce downtime and attract quality tenants.

Effective property management also involves staying updated on legal obligations and compliance requirements related to rental properties to mitigate any potential legal issues.

When you establish property management systems and processes, efficiently manage tenants and maintenance, and optimize rental income and property performance, you will safeguard your investments, maximize returns, and cultivate positive landlord-tenant relationships.

Chapter 9

Potential Risks in Real Estate

Mitigating risks in real estate investments is of utmost importance to protect one's investment and ensure long-term success. I have built a great portfolio in real estate and I can tell you for a fact that this is a highly risk-taking sector.

Real estate investments are not without risks, but by identifying, assessing, and implementing strategies to manage these risks, investors can minimize potential pitfalls and maximize returns. Let's delve into each aspect in more detail:

To effectively mitigate risks, you need to identify and assess the potential risks associated with their real estate investments. This involves a comprehensive evaluation of various factors, including:

a. Market Risk: Real estate markets are subject to fluctuations influenced by economic conditions, interest rates, supply and demand dynamics, and demographic trends. Understanding these market forces and their potential impact on property values and rental demand is essential.

b. Financial Risk: Poor financial planning, excessive debt, or inadequate cash flow management can result in financial instability and an inability to cover expenses or mortgage payments. Thorough financial analysis, accurate cash flow projections, and contingency planning are critical to mitigate financial risks.

c. Property Risk: Properties are exposed to various risks, including physical damage, natural disasters, or unexpected maintenance issues. Assessing the condition of the property, conducting thorough inspections, and considering potential risks related to the location, construction quality, and age of the property can help identify and mitigate property-related risks.

d. Legal and Regulatory Risk: Real estate investments are subject to legal and regulatory requirements that can change over time. Understanding local laws, zoning regulations, building codes, and tenant rights is essential to ensure compliance and avoid legal disputes or penalties.

e. Tenant Risk: Tenants can pose risks such as rental payment defaults, property damage, or lease violations. Implementing thorough tenant screening processes, including background checks, credit assessments, and rental history verification, can help minimize tenant-related risks.

Implementing Risk Management Strategies

Once potential risks are identified, investors can implement a range of strategies to mitigate them effectively. Some key risk management strategies include:

a. Diversification: Spreading investments across different property types, locations, or investment strategies can help minimize the impact of market fluctuations. Diversification provides a level of protection by reducing exposure to a single property or market.

b. Due Diligence: Conducting comprehensive due diligence is crucial before acquiring a property. This includes conducting property inspections, evaluating financial records, assessing market conditions, and investigating potential liabilities or legal issues. Thorough due diligence helps uncover any hidden risks or challenges associated with the property.

c. Financial Planning and Analysis: Developing a solid financial plan is essential for mitigating financial risks. This includes accurately projecting cash flows, accounting for vacancies and maintenance expenses, and maintaining sufficient reserves for unexpected costs. Regular financial analysis and monitoring enable proactive risk management.

d. Professional Advisors: Seeking guidance from real estate professionals, legal advisors, and financial experts can provide valuable insights and help navigate complex regulations and legal obligations. Experienced professionals can offer expert advice on investment strategies, risk assessment, and legal compliance.

e. Risk Assessment and Mitigation Strategies: Each property may have specific risks that require tailored mitigation strategies. For example, implementing preventive maintenance measures to minimize property risks, conducting regular property inspections, and promptly addressing maintenance issues can help prevent costly repairs or damages. Thorough tenant screening processes, including background checks and reference verification, can reduce the risk of tenant-related issues.

Insurance Options and Property Security Measures

Insurance plays a vital role in mitigating risks in real estate investments. Understanding the available insurance options and selecting appropriate coverage is crucial. Some key insurance options to consider include:

a. Property Insurance: Property insurance protects against physical damage to the property caused by fire, natural disasters, vandalism, or other covered perils. It provides financial coverage to repair or rebuild the property.

b. Liability Insurance: Liability insurance is a crucial component of understanding insurance options and property security measures in real estate investing. It provides protection against potential legal claims or liabilities arising from injuries or property damage that occur on the property. Liability insurance is designed to cover the costs associated with legal defense, settlements, or judgments if the property owner is found liable for an accident or incident.

c. Rent Loss Insurance: Rent loss insurance provides coverage for lost rental income in case of tenant default, property damage, or other covered events that result in rental income disruptions. This coverage can help mitigate the financial impact of vacancies or rental income interruptions.

d. Title Insurance: Title insurance protects against potential ownership disputes, undisclosed liens, or title defects that may arise during the property acquisition. It provides assurance that the title is clear and protects the investor's ownership rights.

Understanding property security measures is also essential for mitigating risks. Implementing adequate security measures can help protect the property and its occupants, reduce the likelihood of theft or vandalism, and enhance tenant safety and satisfaction. Some security measures to consider include:

a. Physical Security: Installing security systems, surveillance cameras, and proper lighting can deter criminal activities and improve the overall security of the property. This includes securing entrances, common areas, and parking areas.

b. Access Control: Implementing access control measures such as keyless entry systems, electronic gates, or security guards can restrict unauthorized entry and enhance the safety and security of the property.

c. Maintenance and Repairs: Timely maintenance and repairs of security-related features such as locks, doors, windows, and alarm systems are crucial to ensure they are functioning properly and provide the intended security.

d. Emergency Preparedness: Having emergency plans in place, including fire safety measures, evacuation procedures, and contact information for emergency services, is vital to protect the property and its occupants in case of emergencies.

By understanding and implementing appropriate insurance coverage and property security measures, you can mitigate potential risks, protect your investment, and minimize financial losses in the event of unforeseen circumstances.

Chapter 10

Scaling Up Your Portfolio

Scaling up real estate portfolio is a natural progression for many investors seeking to expand their wealth and diversify their holdings. It involves implementing strategies to grow your investments, exploring different property sectors, and effectively managing multiple properties and portfolios. Let's delve into each aspect in more detail:

Some strategies for scaling up and diversifying your real estate investments are:

a. Incremental Growth: One strategy for scaling up is to gradually acquire additional properties over time. This can be achieved by reinvesting profits from existing properties or leveraging financing options to fund new acquisitions. Incremental growth allows for controlled expansion while minimizing financial risks.

b. Joint Ventures and Partnerships: Collaborating with other investors through joint ventures or partnerships can facilitate larger-scale investments and provide access to additional resources and expertise. Joint ventures can involve pooling financial resources, sharing risks, and leveraging each other's networks and skills to pursue more significant investment opportunities.

c. Real Estate Investment Trusts (REITs): Investing in REITs is another way to diversify and scale up your real estate portfolio. REITs are companies that own, operate, or finance income-generating real estate. By purchasing shares in a REIT, investors can gain exposure to a diverse range of properties across various sectors without the need to directly own or manage individual properties.

d. Geographic Expansion: Exploring new markets and geographic areas can provide opportunities for portfolio expansion. Conducting thorough market research, analyzing economic indicators, and assessing growth potential are crucial when considering new locations. Investing in different regions or countries can offer diversification and potentially higher returns.

e. Property Development and Renovation: Engaging in property development or renovation projects can be an effective strategy for scaling up. By identifying properties with value-add potential, investors can increase the property's value through renovations, upgrades, or redevelopment. This approach requires careful analysis, project management skills, and a solid understanding of the local market dynamics.

Exploring Commercial and Residential Property Sectors

Imagine you're considering investing in different types of properties, and you have two main options: commercial properties and residential properties. Let's break down what each option entails:

a. Commercial Properties: Investing in commercial properties is like owning buildings that are used for business purposes. These can include office buildings, shopping centers, warehouses, or factories. It's like buying a property and then renting it out to businesses, just like a landlord would rent out a space to a store or a company.

Commercial properties can be attractive because they often generate higher rental income compared to residential properties. It's like receiving a higher monthly rent from a store than you would from an apartment. Additionally, commercial leases are typically long-term agreements, which means that businesses rent the space for several years. This provides a stable and predictable income stream for the property owner.

However, investing in commercial properties may require a higher initial investment. It's like needing more money upfront to purchase a shopping center compared to buying a residential property. Commercial properties can also involve longer lease negotiation periods, as businesses may have specific requirements or negotiation processes.

Lastly, managing commercial properties requires expertise in tenant management and lease administration. It's like having knowledge and experience in dealing with businesses, their needs, and the legal aspects of commercial leases.

    b. Residential Properties: Investing in residential properties is like owning homes or apartments that are used for people to live in. These can include single-family homes, duplexes, apartment buildings, or condominiums. It's like buying a property and then renting it out to individuals or families, just like a landlord would rent out an apartment to tenants.

Residential properties are popular among real estate investors because they provide a steady stream of rental income and the potential for property value appreciation over time. It's like receiving monthly rent from tenants living in your rental properties and also having the possibility that the value of the property increases in the future.

Compared to commercial properties, residential properties generally have lower entry barriers. It's like needing less money upfront to buy a house or an apartment compared to a large office building. Residential properties also offer more flexibility in terms of property management and tenant turnover. It's like having the freedom to choose how to manage the property and being able to find new tenants more easily if one decides to move out.

When deciding between commercial and residential properties, it's important to consider factors such as the initial investment required, rental income potential, lease durations, and management expertise. Understanding the differences between these two sectors can help you make informed decisions about which type of property investment suits your goals and resources.

Managing Multiple Properties and Portfolios

a. Property Management Systems: Efficient property management systems and processes are crucial when managing multiple properties. Implementing standardized procedures for tenant screening, lease administration, rent collection, maintenance requests, and property inspections can help streamline operations and ensure consistent performance across properties.

b. Delegating Responsibilities: As your real estate portfolio grows, it may become necessary to delegate certain responsibilities to professionals such as property managers, accountants, or legal advisors. Outsourcing tasks like property maintenance, tenant communication, financial management, and legal compliance can alleviate the burden of managing multiple properties and allow you to focus on strategic decision-making.

c. Scalable Infrastructure: Building a scalable infrastructure is essential for managing multiple properties efficiently. This includes adopting property management software, establishing effective communication channels with tenants, maintaining accurate financial records, and implementing reporting mechanisms to track the performance of each property and portfolio as a whole.

d. Portfolio Performance Analysis: Regularly analyzing the performance of your properties and portfolios is critical for identifying areas of improvement, evaluating returns, and making informed decisions. This involves monitoring key performance indicators (KPIs) such as occupancy rates, rental income, expenses, cash flow, and investment yields.

By conducting periodic portfolio reviews, investors can identify underperforming assets, assess the overall portfolio balance, and make adjustments as needed, such as divesting from underperforming properties or reallocating resources to properties with higher growth potential.

e. Risk Management: Managing risks becomes increasingly important when dealing with multiple properties. This includes maintaining adequate insurance coverage for each property, conducting regular property inspections to identify potential hazards or maintenance issues, and staying informed about legal and regulatory requirements in each jurisdiction where properties are located. Implementing risk mitigation strategies and contingency plans can help protect the portfolio from unforeseen events and minimize potential losses.

f. Portfolio Diversification: Diversifying your real estate portfolio across different property types, locations, and market sectors can help mitigate risk and enhance overall returns. By having a mix of residential and commercial properties, properties in different geographical areas, or properties with varying lease terms, investors can reduce their exposure to specific market fluctuations and capitalize on diverse income streams.

g. Professional Networks and Relationships: As your portfolio expands, building a strong network of real estate professionals, including brokers, property managers, contractors, and legal advisors, becomes increasingly valuable. These relationships can provide access to market insights, investment opportunities, and reliable service providers, ultimately facilitating the smooth management and growth of your portfolio.

In conclusion, scaling up your real estate portfolio involves implementing effective strategies, exploring different property sectors, and efficiently managing multiple properties and portfolios. Gradual growth, partnerships, and diversification can contribute to portfolio expansion, while efficient property management systems, delegation of responsibilities, and scalable infrastructure are crucial for successful portfolio management.

Additionally, conducting thorough market research, managing risks, and regularly reviewing portfolio performance are vital elements in achieving long-term success and maximizing returns in the real estate industry.

Chapter 11

Exit Strategies

Real estate investment exit strategies are an important aspect of any investment plan. They involve determining the best course of action for selling or transferring ownership of properties to maximize returns and ensure long-term wealth preservation. Let's discuss the key elements of real estate investment exit strategies in detail:

Imagine you're playing a game and you have a plan for how you will finish and exit the game. Exit strategies in real estate investments are similar. They refer to the methods or plans that investors have for finishing or disposing of their real estate investments. These strategies are usually thought about at the beginning of the investment and can vary depending on the investor's goals, market conditions, and how long they plan to invest. Here are some common exit strategies:

a. Sale: The most straightforward exit strategy is selling the property on the open market. It's like finishing the game and selling your game pieces or cards to other players. Investors may choose to sell the property when they have achieved their desired return on investment, when market conditions are favorable, or when they need to convert the property into cash.

b. 1031 Exchange: In the United States, a 1031 exchange is like a special rule that allows investors to defer paying capital gains taxes when they sell one property and reinvest the proceeds into another similar property. It's like trading your game piece for a different one without having to pay any taxes. This strategy can be advantageous for investors who want to preserve their wealth and take advantage of tax benefits while transitioning into a new investment.

c. Refinancing: Instead of selling the property, investors may choose to refinance their existing mortgage. It's like modifying the rules of the game to access more resources or to make it easier to play. By refinancing, investors can extract some of the equity they've built up in the property or get lower interest rates on their mortgage. This strategy allows them to access cash while still keeping ownership of the property.

d. Lease Options: Offering lease options to potential buyers is like giving them a chance to play the game and eventually buy the property. This involves leasing the property to a tenant with the option for the tenant to purchase the property at a later date. It's like letting someone borrow your game piece for a while and giving them the option to buy it from you later. This strategy can be useful when market conditions are not favorable for an immediate sale.

e. Wealth Transfer: Just like you can pass on your games or toys to your siblings or friends, investors may choose to transfer ownership of their properties to their heirs or beneficiaries. This can be done through legal arrangements like trusts, wills, or other estate planning methods. It ensures that the property and wealth are preserved and can be passed down to future generations to continue owning and benefiting from the property.

These exit strategies provide investors with different options for finishing their real estate investments based on their goals and the circumstances at hand. Just as having a plan for exiting a game can be important, having a well-thought-out exit strategy can help investors make informed decisions and maximize the returns on their real estate investments.

Assessing Options for Property Disposal or Wealth Transfer

Considering property disposal or wealth transfer is like having a valuable possession, like a rare collectible or a piece of jewelry, and you're considering how and when to sell it or transfer it to someone else. There are a few important factors you need to consider:

a. Market Conditions: Just like you would consider the current demand and prices for your valuable possession, it's important to assess the current market conditions when deciding to sell or transfer a property. Factors like supply and demand, interest rates, and economic indicators can affect how much your property is worth and how easy it will be to find a buyer or transfer it to someone else.

b. Financial Considerations: When thinking about selling or transferring a property, you need to evaluate the financial aspects of your investment. This includes considering how much the property has appreciated in value over time, the cash flow it generates (such as rental income), and the potential tax implications. You should calculate your return on investment and consult with financial advisors to understand the financial impact of different options and make informed decisions.

c. Investor Goals and Objectives: Everyone has different goals when it comes to their investments. Some people may want to make a quick profit and prefer to sell the property as soon as possible. Others may prioritize long-term wealth preservation and choose strategies that involve holding onto the property or transferring ownership to family members or beneficiaries. It's important to understand your own goals and objectives so that you can choose the exit strategy that aligns with them.

d. Legal and Tax Considerations: Selling or transferring a property involves legal and tax implications. It's important to consult with legal and tax advisors who can guide you through the process. They can help you understand the tax implications, plan for estate transfers, and ensure that you comply with local laws and regulations. They will provide valuable advice on how to structure the transaction in a way that minimizes tax burdens and protects your interests.

When you consider all these, you can make informed decisions when it comes to selling or transferring your property. Just as you would carefully consider the timing and potential buyers when selling a valuable possession, assessing these factors will help you choose the best option for disposing of your property or transferring your wealth.

Maximizing Returns and Planning for Long-Term Wealth Preservation

Imagine you have a garden where you grow different types of plants. To make the most out of your garden and ensure its long-term success, there are a few important things you need to consider. The same goes for maximizing returns and planning for long-term wealth preservation. To achieve this, you should consider:

a. **Evaluating Property Performance**: Just like you would regularly assess how well your plants are growing, it's important to continuously monitor the performance of your properties. This includes looking at factors like rental income, occupancy rates, and expenses. Regular evaluations help you identify areas for improvement and determine if your properties are aligned with your long-term investment goals.

b. **Optimizing Your Portfolio:** In your garden, you would want a mix of different plants to create a beautiful and balanced landscape. Similarly, in real estate investing, it's important to assess the overall composition of your portfolio and adjust the allocation of resources. This involves reviewing the performance of each property within your portfolio, identifying any underperforming assets, and considering strategies like selling or repositioning to improve the overall performance of your portfolio.

c. **Market Analysis**: Just as you would keep an eye on gardening trends and weather patterns, conducting thorough market analysis is crucial for long-term wealth preservation. This means understanding market trends, changes in demographics, and economic indicators. By staying informed about market dynamics, you can make informed decisions about when to hold onto properties or sell them to maximize returns.

d. **Diversification**: In your garden, you wouldn't want to plant only one type of plant, as it could be vulnerable to pests or diseases. Similarly, in real estate investing, diversifying your portfolio is important. This means investing in different property types (residential, commercial, industrial), different locations, and different market sectors. By spreading your investments, you reduce the risk of being overly reliant on one market and increase your chances of capturing opportunities in diverse markets.

e. **Long-Term Financial Planning**: Just like you have a plan for maintaining and nurturing your garden for years to come, real estate investments should be part of a broader financial plan. This involves considering factors like retirement planning, cash flow requirements, and transferring wealth to future generations. By integrating your real estate investments into a comprehensive financial plan, you can ensure that your investments contribute to long-term wealth preservation.

f. **Professional Guidance**: Just as you might consult with gardening experts or landscapers for advice, seeking guidance from real estate professionals, financial advisors, and legal experts is valuable. These professionals can provide insights into market conditions, tax implications, estate planning, and investment strategies that align with your goals and objectives.

When you implement these effective exit strategies and consider long-term financial planning, you can ensure the successful realization of your real estate investments and safeguard your wealth for the future.

Chapter 12

Sustainability In Real Estate

Building a sustainable real estate fortune goes beyond financial success. It involves incorporating sustainability and ethical practices, contributing to community development and social impact, and leaving a legacy through responsible real estate investment practices.

Incorporating Sustainability and Ethical Practices involves:

a. Environmental Sustainability: When it comes to real estate investing, considering the environment and taking steps to minimize negative impacts is important. It's like being mindful of the resources you use and making efforts to reduce waste in your everyday life.

In real estate, this means choosing eco-friendly building materials, using renewable energy sources like solar power, conserving water, and managing waste responsibly. By incorporating these practices, investors can create properties that are environmentally friendly and promote energy efficiency.

b. Social Responsibility: Ethical practices in real estate involve prioritizing the well-being of communities and the people affected by the investments. It's similar to treating others with fairness, respect, and consideration in our daily interactions. In real estate, this means practicing fair housing, which means not discriminating against anyone based on factors like race, religion, or gender.

It also means conducting business in an ethical manner, being responsible and responsive to tenants' needs, and supporting initiatives that improve the quality of life for residents. For example, investing in affordable housing projects or community development programs can be part of social responsibility in real estate.

c. Governance and Transparency: Building a sustainable real estate fortune requires following good practices and being transparent in business operations. It's like having clear rules and being honest in your interactions with others.

In real estate, this involves conducting thorough research and due diligence before making investments, complying with legal and regulatory requirements, and being transparent in financial reporting. By establishing strong governance structures, maintaining accurate records, and communicating openly with stakeholders, investors can build trust and credibility.

Incorporating sustainability and ethical practices in real estate investing means being mindful of the environmental impact, considering the well-being of communities and stakeholders, and conducting business with integrity and transparency. By doing so, investors can make a positive contribution to society and build a sustainable real estate portfolio.

Contributing to Community Development and Social Impact

As much as real estate investing is concerned, you must contribute your quota in ensuring development in the community where your assets are situated. Some ways you can do this include:

   a. Affordable Housing: Real estate investors have the opportunity to make a positive impact on communities by investing in affordable housing projects. Affordable housing means providing homes that are safe and reasonably priced for people who may struggle to find suitable housing options. This is part of what we do at Wisdom Kwati Smart City.

By investing in these projects, you can help address the housing needs of underserved populations, such as low-income families or individuals. This contributes to social equality and ensures that everyone has access to a decent place to live.

b. Job Creation and Economic Growth: Real estate investments can have a ripple effect on the local economy by creating job opportunities. When investors develop or renovate properties, they often require the services of architects, construction workers, plumbers, electricians, and many others.

This stimulates economic growth and provides employment opportunities for local residents. By supporting job creation, real estate investors contribute to the overall prosperity of the community and create sustainable long-term benefits.

c. Social Infrastructure: Real estate investments can go beyond just housing and have a broader impact on communities. Investors can choose to invest in projects that enhance social infrastructure, such as schools, healthcare facilities, parks, and community centers. By improving these aspects of a community, investors contribute to the well-being and quality of life of its residents.

For example, investing in a new school can provide children with better educational opportunities, while investing in healthcare facilities can improve access to medical services.

When you contribute to community development and social impact through real estate investing, you play a role in creating a more equitable society, fostering economic growth, and enhancing the overall livability of communities.

Leaving a Legacy As An Investor

Most people don't invest for the long-term thus, they don't think LEGACY when investing. It is important that you invest responsibly in real estate and think about leaving a legacy each time you invest. Here are ways to achieve this:

a. Long-Term Value Creation: Responsible real estate investors focus on creating lasting value through their investments. They carefully choose properties that have the potential to grow in value over time.

Factors such as location, market demand, and future growth prospects are considered when making investment decisions.

By investing in properties that appreciate in value, investors aim to create a lasting legacy for future generations. This means that the investments they make today can continue to benefit their families or communities in the future.

b. Philanthropy and Giving Back: Responsible real estate investors understand the importance of giving back to society. They allocate a portion of their resources towards philanthropic initiatives that align with their values. This can involve supporting charitable organizations, funding education programs, or contributing to community development projects.

By using their financial resources to make a positive impact, real estate investors leave a meaningful legacy beyond their property investments. They aim to create a better world by supporting causes and projects that are important to them.

c. Education and Mentorship: Real estate investors who are committed to leaving a legacy also focus on sharing their knowledge and expertise. They understand the value of education and mentorship in shaping the future of the industry. Seasoned investors can provide guidance, share educational resources, or act as mentors to aspiring real estate investors.

By empowering others with the knowledge and tools to succeed, these investors leave a legacy of mentorship and contribute to the development of future professionals in the field.

When you incorporate responsible real estate investment practices, such as long-term value creation, philanthropy, and education, you can leave a lasting legacy that extends beyond your property investments. This will help create positive change, support important causes, and empower others to succeed in the industry.

Conclusion

Kwame's journey from a young dreamer to a successful real estate magnate was a testament to the power of passion, knowledge, perseverance, and social responsibility. Through his unwavering commitment to ethical business practices and community upliftment, he had not only built a real estate fortune but also transformed countless lives and communities across Africa.

Kwame's story became an inspiration to aspiring real estate entrepreneurs across the continent. His success was a beacon of hope, demonstrating that with dedication, hard work, and a strong sense of purpose, one could make a profound impact on the world.

As his organization flourished, Kwame's vision of creating a vibrant learning community for real estate enthusiasts became a reality. The organization attracted talented individuals from diverse backgrounds, fostering an environment of collaboration, innovation, and shared growth.

Through the organization's initiatives, aspiring real estate entrepreneurs received guidance, mentorship, and access to valuable resources. They developed the necessary skills and knowledge to navigate the complexities of the real estate industry, while also imbibing the values of social responsibility and ethical practices.

The impact of Kwame's work extended far beyond the realm of real estate. His community development projects had revitalized neglected areas, creating sustainable and inclusive neighborhoods where residents could thrive. The vocational training programs he supported had empowered individuals with valuable skills, opening up new opportunities for employment and economic growth.

As Kwame's real estate empire expanded, he remained rooted in his vision of using his wealth and influence to uplift others. He continued to invest in education and vocational training programs, supporting initiatives that aimed to bridge the opportunity gap and empower young individuals to pursue their dreams.

Kwame's commitment to environmental sustainability also remained steadfast. He consistently integrated green building practices into his projects, setting an example for the industry and advocating for environmentally conscious development.

The legacy of Kwame's work was not limited to his lifetime. The impact he had made and the principles he had instilled within his organization continued to shape the African real estate landscape for generations to come. As his mentees and followers carried forward his vision, they contributed to the growth and progress of the industry, each making their unique mark on the continent.

Kwame's story was celebrated as a testament to what was possible when passion, knowledge, and social responsibility converged. His journey stood as a reminder that success in the real estate industry was not solely measured by financial gains but by the transformative impact one could have on individuals, communities, and the broader society.

As Kwame looked out over the city he had helped shape, he felt a deep sense of fulfillment. His dream of becoming a real estate entrepreneur had not only come true but had exceeded his wildest expectations. He had built a real estate fortune, transformed communities, empowered individuals, and left a lasting legacy of prosperity and progress.

And as he contemplated the future, Kwame knew that his journey was far from over. There were still countless neighborhoods to revitalize, aspiring entrepreneurs to mentor, and social and environmental challenges to address. With unwavering determination and a heart full of purpose, he embraced the next chapter of his real estate odyssey, ready to continue making a difference and shaping the African real estate landscape for years to come.

You too can become a Kwame.

The ball is in your court.

Real Estate Glossary

Real Estate: Refers to property consisting of land and any improvements on it, such as buildings, structures, natural resources, and other tangible assets.

Property: A piece of real estate or land that is owned or controlled by an individual, organization, or entity.

Asset: Something of value that is owned and can be used to generate income or provide a financial benefit, such as real estate properties.

Ownership: The legal right to possess, control, and dispose of a property or real estate asset.

Title: Legal ownership and rights to a property or real estate asset, typically documented through a title deed.

Deed: A legal document that transfers ownership of a property from one party to another.

Mortgage: A loan obtained from a financial institution to finance the purchase of a property, where the property itself serves as collateral.

Equity: The difference between the market value of a property and the outstanding balance on any loans or mortgages secured against it.

Rental Income: The income received from leasing or renting out a property to tenants.

Lease: A legal agreement between a property owner (landlord) and a tenant, specifying the terms and conditions of renting the property.

Property Management: The management and administration of real estate properties on behalf of owners, including tasks such as tenant selection, rent collection, maintenance, and repairs.

Appraisal: The process of determining the value of a property based on various factors, such as location, condition, size, and comparable sales.

Capital Appreciation: An increase in the value of a property over time, resulting in potential gains for the owner when selling or refinancing the property.

Cash Flow: The net income generated by a property after deducting expenses, such as mortgage payments, property taxes, insurance, and maintenance costs.

Market Analysis: The evaluation of real estate market conditions, trends, and factors that can affect property values, demand, and supply.

Commercial Property: Real estate properties used for business purposes, such as office buildings, retail spaces, and industrial facilities.

Residential Property: Real estate properties used for residential purposes, including houses, apartments, condominiums, and townhouses.

Development: The process of improving or modifying a property, such as constructing new buildings, renovating existing structures, or changing land use.

ROI (Return on Investment): A financial metric used to measure the profitability of an investment, including real estate, by comparing the return or profit generated to the initial investment.

Foreclosure: The legal process through which a lender takes possession of a property from a borrower who has defaulted on mortgage payments.

Landlord: The owner of a property who leases or rents it to a tenant in exchange for rent payments.

Tenant: An individual or entity who rents or leases a property from a landlord.

Property Tax: Taxes levied by local governments on the value of real estate properties, typically used to fund public services and infrastructure.

Escrow: The holding of funds, documents, or assets by a third party in a real estate transaction until specified conditions are met.

Zoning: The process of dividing land into different zones or areas for specific purposes, such as residential, commercial, or industrial use, regulated by local zoning laws.

Homeowners Association (HOA): A governing body or organization that manages and enforces rules and regulations for a community or housing development.

Land Survey: The measurement and mapping of a property's boundaries, features, and topography, conducted by a licensed surveyor.

Closing Costs: The fees and expenses incurred during the final stages of a real estate transaction, such as appraisal fees, title search fees, attorney fees, and insurance premiums.

Real Estate Agent: A licensed professional who assists buyers and sellers in real estate transactions, providing services such as property listings, property showings, negotiation, and paperwork.

Comparative Market Analysis (CMA): An evaluation of similar properties in the same area to determine the market value of a property, often used by real estate agents to help sellers set an appropriate listing price.

Down Payment: The initial upfront payment made by a buyer toward the purchase of a property, typically a percentage of the total purchase price.

Capitalization Rate (Cap Rate): A ratio used to estimate the potential return on a real estate investment, calculated by dividing the property's net operating income by its purchase price or value.

Depreciation: The decrease in the value of a property over time due to factors such as wear and tear, age, and market conditions.

Easement: The right to use or access a specific portion of someone else's property for a particular purpose, such as a shared driveway or utility lines.

Home Inspection: A thorough examination of a property's condition, structure, and systems, conducted by a professional inspector to identify any potential issues or defects.

Short Sale: The sale of a property for an amount lower than the outstanding mortgage balance, typically arranged with the lender's approval when the borrower is facing financial hardship.

1031 Exchange: A tax-deferred exchange that allows real estate investors to sell a property and reinvest the proceeds into a similar property, deferring capital gains taxes.

Conveyancing: The legal process of transferring ownership of a property from a seller to a buyer, including the preparation and execution of necessary documents.

Fair Housing Act: A federal law that prohibits discrimination in housing based on factors such as race, color, religion, sex, national origin, disability, and familial status.

Land Use: The purpose for which a particular parcel of land is designated, such as residential, commercial, agricultural, or recreational use, regulated by zoning and land-use regulations.

Real Estate Bubble: A period of rapid and unsustainable increase in real estate prices, followed by a sharp decline or burst, often associated with speculative buying and excessive lending.

Landlord-Tenant Laws: Legal regulations that govern the rights and responsibilities of landlords and tenants in rental agreements, including issues such as rent increases, eviction processes, and tenant protections.

Rent-to-Own: A lease agreement that includes an option for the tenant to purchase the property at a predetermined price within a specified period.

Gross Rent Multiplier (GRM): A ratio used to estimate the value of an income-generating property by dividing the property's sale price by its annual rental income.

Due Diligence: The process of conducting thorough research and investigation to assess the potential risks, financial viability, and legal aspects of a real estate investment before finalizing the transaction.

Real Estat Syndication: The pooling of funds from multiple investors to invest in larger real estate projects, allowing investors to access opportunities they may not be able to pursue individually.

Real Estate Wholesaling: A strategy in which an investor finds distressed properties at a discounted price and assigns the contract to another buyer for a fee, without actually taking ownership of the property.

Real Estate Investment Group: An organization or entity that pools funds from multiple investors to collectively invest in real estate properties, sharing profits and risks.

Market Value: The estimated price at which a property would sell between a willing buyer and seller in the current market conditions.

Real Estate Portfolio: A collection of multiple real estate investments owned by an individual or entity, providing diversification and potentially higher returns.

Cash-on-Cash Return: A measure of the annual return on investment generated by a property, calculated by dividing the property's net operating income by the initial cash investment.

Off-Plan Property: A property that is purchased before its construction or completion, based on the developer's plans and specifications.

Real Estate Development: The process of acquiring, improving, and constructing real estate projects, such as residential communities, commercial buildings, or mixed-use developments.

Gross Income: The total income generated by a property before deducting expenses, including rental income, parking fees, and any additional sources of revenue.

Net Operating Income (NOI): The income generated by a property after deducting operating expenses, such as property taxes, insurance, maintenance costs, and property management fees.

Portfolio Diversification: The strategy of spreading investments across different types of real estate properties, locations, and markets to reduce risk and optimize returns.

Market Rent: The current rental value of a property in the prevailing real estate market conditions, determined by factors such as location, property type, and demand.

Due Diligence Period: The specified timeframe during a real estate transaction in which the buyer investigates and verifies the property's condition, financials, legal status, and other relevant aspects.

Property Flipping: The practice of purchasing a property with the intention of reselling it quickly for a profit, often involving renovations or improvements to increase its value.

Absorption Rate: The rate at which available properties are sold or leased in a particular market over a specified period, indicating the pace of market activity and demand.

Operating Expenses: The costs incurred to maintain, manage, and operate a property, including utilities, repairs, maintenance, property taxes, insurance, and property management fees.

Rental Yield: The annual income generated by a property as a percentage of its purchase price or value, indicating the return on investment from rental income.

Real Estate Syndicator: An individual or company that facilitates real estate syndication by identifying investment opportunities, raising capital from investors, and managing the investment.

Real Estate Market Analysis: The process of evaluating market conditions, trends, and economic factors that impact real estate values, demand, and investment opportunities.

Due-on-Sale Clause: A provision in a mortgage agreement that allows the lender to demand full repayment of the loan if the property is sold or transferred to a new owner.

Capital Stack: The hierarchy of financing sources used to fund a real estate project, including equity investments, mezzanine loans, and senior debt.

Exit Strategy: A planned approach for selling or disposing of a real estate investment to realize the desired returns, mitigate risks, or accommodate changes in investment objectives.

Real Estate Bubble: A speculative market phenomenon characterized by rapid and unsustainable increases in property prices, followed by a sharp decline or market correction.

Real Estate Cycle: The recurring pattern of ups and downs in real estate market conditions, influenced by factors such as economic cycles, supply and demand dynamics, and investor sentiment.

Real Estate Investment Analysis: The process of evaluating the financial feasibility and potential returns of a real estate investment by analyzing factors such as cash flow projections, income and expenses, and property appreciation.

These terms and their meanings form a comprehensive vocabulary register for understanding and discussing various aspects of real estate. Familiarity with these terms can help you navigate the real estate industry more effectively and make informed decisions.

Thank you for reading.

I would love to get your feedback about this book.

Send an email to wisdomkwati@gmail.com